Stations

Chris van Uffelen

Stations

BRAUN

CONTENTS

Stations, a track record

by Chris van Uffelen

Despite their 180-year history, stations are a relatively new form of architecture. After the invention of passenger transportation on rails – mine cars moved by stationary steam engines were already used in mining earlier – the first representative examples of the genre were initially based on postal stops, such as at the Stockton-Darlington line (1822–1825). At the first railroad station in today's sense of the word, the Crown Street Station in Liverpool, which was created in 1830 as part of the railroad track to Manchester, the reception building was still at the longitudinal side, while a wooden hall protected the platform area along the track to Manchester. The history of railroad stations thus began with a transit station in which the reception area and the hall were separate buildings. This division of stations into two buildings, of which one is primarily representative and the other for engineering purposes remained the only architectural option for a long time and has not disappeared to this day. In the 1830s and the following decades, railroads initially spread across the rest of Europe and the USA, then into the countries that were colonized by these nations. The postal manor houses, the duty or customs stations of the pre-industrial area, remained the dominant prototype, while the hall and the main building continued to be built separately as in Liverpool. Frequently, two buildings, for arrivals and departures respectively, faced each other with the roofed platform area located between them. In the course of the second half of the 19th century, the two individual buildings were linked by a transverse reception hall, which evolved into the main section of the terminal station. Through its large-scale enclosure, the hall between the three building sections increasingly evolved into a section of a single building, in other words a roofed cour d'honneur of an upended castle. John Dobson's Central Station in Newcastle, the first fully roofed station, was built in 1853, one year before the Crystal Pallace (extended in the 1890s by William Bell).

//

However, as opposed to the cour d'honneur, the main view of the station was the façade of the service and lobby section that faced the city. The large terminal stations were often modeled after palaces or other large buildings derived from the thematic architecture of ancient Rome or triumphal archs. Depending on the country or the region all historically available styles were applied. Similar to the cross-sectional façade of sacral buildings, they reflected the room structures located behind them, while their towers (bearing clocks or containing water reservoirs) also stood out in the cityscape similar to a church. Behind the façades also, in the halls in front of the cour references to church architecture are omnipresent, as this building style was the only one to resort to that featured large open room structures, whether as halls or as basilica, unless the designers wanted to resort to the antiquity era (Pennsylvania Station by McKim, Mead and White in New York, 1904–1910). Large stations like these were usually built at the outskirts of town of their respective eras and were highlighted in terms of urban planning through axes and new streets. This highlighting of the new "cathedrals" was already implemented in the propyleum located in front of the Eustan Station in London by

↖ | **Jakob Ignaz Hittorf,** Gare du Nord, Paris, 1861–1865
← | **Paul Bonatz,** Hauptbahnhof Stuttgart, 1911–1928

→ | **Giovanni Michelucci with Gruppo Toscano**, Stazione di Firenze Santa Maria Novella, 1933–1935
→→| **Otto Wagner,** Karlsplatzstation Stadtbahn Vienna, 1898
↘ | **Piere Luigi Nervi,** Stazione Termini, Rome, 1938–1955
↘↘ | **Agence des Gares SNCF, Jean-Marie Duthilleul, Etienne Tricaud,** extension Gare du Nord, Paris, 2002

Richard Hardwick, designed in the Doric classicism style. The Gare du Nord of Paris (Jacob Ignaz Hittorf, 1861–1865) and the central station of Frankfurt / Main (Hermann Eggert, 1883–1888) are typical examples of the assimilation of various styles in the new construction projects. It was only rarely possible to extend tracks to the city center, as in Amsterdam, where the central station (P. J. H. Cuypers, 1877–1889) is located on an artificial island at the mouth of the Amstel in the river IJ – right at the center of the historic concentric city structure. Applying a mixture of Gothic and Renaissance, the architect attempted to apply the most popular styles of the time in a modern pastiche in the presumed typical national mix of ashlars and brick. However, for smaller transit stations less ostentatious types of buildings were used. The range of shapes of Eclecticist villas was particularly well suited for smaller communities, while their various verandahs and loggias provided good connecting points for platforms. For many of the early tracks, standard building units were created, which were in part modular and could be adjusted to the respective setting. Behind the stone representative wings of the large buildings, the platform halls became increasingly transparent and generously proportioned. The

wooden supports of the early days had long since been replaced by iron beams and the formerly stone side walls became increasingly transparent, further highlighted by the blue half-timbered elements in the St Pancras Station in London (Neo-Gothic reception building by George G. Scott, track hall by H. W. Barlow, 1863–1877).

Extensively glassed halls are also found in the station buildings of the Art Nouveau era, during which asymmetrical-composed facilities were introduced (Eliel Saarinen, station in Helsinki, 1910–1914) and that shaped the style of subway stations in particular. The London underground was already established in 1863, but this form of local transport only achieved a breakthrough until the introduction of electric railway operations. Hector Guimard's Art Nouveau style entrances to the Paris Métro are just as exemplary as those of Otto Wagner to the Vienna metropolitan railway. In Berlin, Alfred Grenander turned from Art Nouveau to early Monumental style around the year 1912, followed by Modernism. The Stuttgart central station, which was implemented by Paul Bonatz starting in 1911 and during the first World War, is a masterpiece of the early Monumental era. On the one hand, its seemingly

immobile cyclopean masonry is a prime example for the megalomania of the time, while on the other hand the sequence of rooms and the additive accumulation of differently shaped buildings were pioneers of a more functional style of stations. The previously increasingly desired closer connection between the reception building and the hall was abandoned during this era in favor of a symbiotic coexistence. In Italy, the S. Maria Novella station in Florence (1933–1935), constructed by the group surrounding Michelucci, with its strictly orthogonal and supported structure became the main building of Rationalism. The building style of subway stations in particular was considerably standardized, not necessarily always resulting in a sober design, as seen by the Art-Déco station by Charles Holden in London from the 1920s to 1930s. The Stalinist subway stations of Moscow from the 1930s are even more extremely decorated, serving as models for subsequent Soviet subway stations in the 1950s.

Following WWII, many main line stations were also created underground as counterparts to the subway stations, such as the Pennsylvania station, which was already implemented at the turn of the century,

a trend that was also present in Tony Garnier's planned industrial city. This freed the above-ground sections from functional shape requirements and many older buildings, especially those dating from the 19th century, were destroyed in the course of the renovation. Frequently, the new buildings were combined with shopping malls, an equally new type of structure in Europe (Forum Les Halles in Paris). Pier Luigi Nervi's Stazione Termini in Rome (1938–1955) clearly exhibits its origins from the pre-World War I era, even though its cubic style is totally in line with post-war modernism.

It was not until the 1970s and the emerging preservation of monuments and historic buildings, that the destruction of facilities from the previous century stopped with the recognition of 19th century architecture in general and the importance of stations as doors to (inner) cities in particular. In that era, subway stations also received more individual designs. The rediscovery of stations in the 1980s was accompanied by a renaissance of the old buildings as central facilities. For example, the Leipzig main station was expanded into a shopping mall by HPP in the second half of the 1990s. This mixed use allowed the

operator to afford the running costs of the previously oversized old buildings. At the same time, the customers – of the shopping mall or the railroad – can enjoy a conglomerated center close to the city with a historic ambiance. Away from the city center or as part of new settlements, new station buildings are created for modern high-speed trains often serving the function of city crowns or central junctions and thus with a highly visible appearance. They are either more condensed than the old stations or include plans for numerous further functions from the outset. Frequently, these monumental structures resemble modern airports in terms of their functionality (optimized traffic ways) and architectural style, and in part also fulfill the same high security requirements. In addition, stations are supposed to offer secure and comfortable places to stay, in which the illumination plays a great part at night. The modern design considerably increases the identification value of the site, even in case of smaller buildings such as the tram waiting cabins in Hanover, constructed prior to the year 2000, while minimizing maintenance costs, also due to greater popular acceptance and subsequent lower vandalism compared to purely functional structures.

↖↖ | **Claude Monet,** arrival of a train at the Gare Saint-Lazare, 1877: The effects of the steam on the light fascinated the impressionists.
↖ | **Hermann Eggert,** Hauptbahnhof Frankfurt / Main, 1861–1865, with three iron halls by Schwedler und Frantz measuring 189 by 186 meters
↑ | **Nicholas Grimshaw and Partners,** Waterloo Station, London, 1990–1993
↗ | ↗↗ | **Despang Architekten,** stations of the Expo-line, Hanover, 2000, similar buildings in different materials along the line
→ | **Jean-Michel Othoniel,** Kiosque des Noctambules, Metro entrance, Paris, 2000
→→| **Tahir,** Lentille Météor St. Lazare, Paris, 2003

Heavy Rail

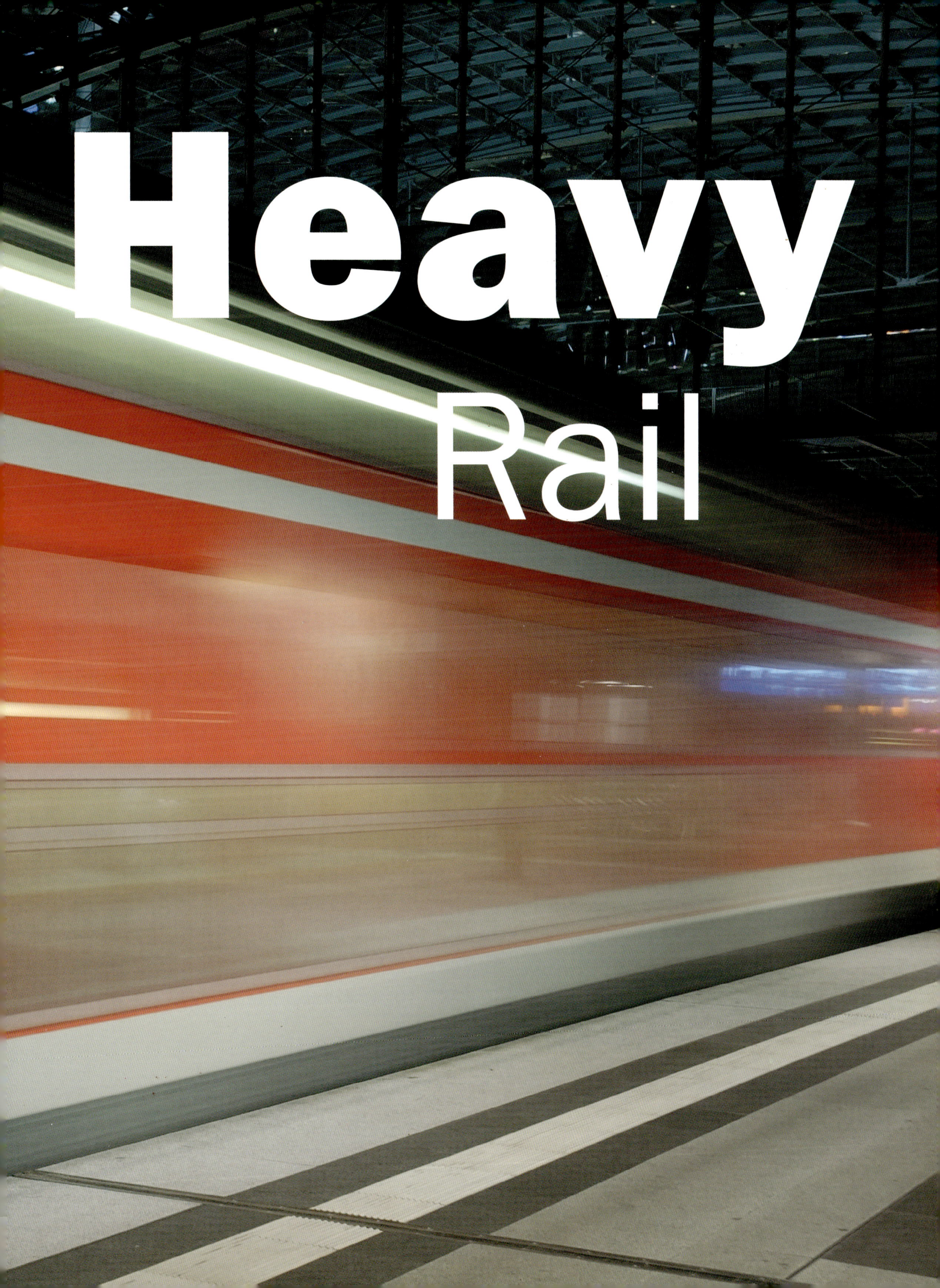

Grimshaw / Keith Brewis,
Mark Middleton

↑ | **Dune-like roof structure**
→ | **Main entrance** at night

Southern Cross station

Melbourne

Southern Cross station is the result of a redevelopment of the old Spencer Street station into a world-class interchange and new landmark for Melbourne. It is the only one of five stations on Melbourne's City Loop to service regional and interstate rail and long-haul bus connections. The expansion of the station allows better transfers between various modes of transport and provides 15 million passengers with fully sheltered and high-quality ticketing, baggage handling and waiting facilities. The design focuses on a dune-like roof, which spans an entire city block to create a cool and shaded civic space that links the Central Business District with the docklands, currently undergoing a regeneration.

PROJECT FACTS

Address: 99 Spencer Street, Docklands, Melbourne, VIC 3008, Australia. **Planning partner:** Jackson Architecture. **Client:** Leighton Contractors. **Completion:** 2007. **Type:** heavy rail. **Number of public levels:** 3. **Number of platforms:** 14. **Number of passengers per day:** 90,000. **Gross floor area:** 60,000 m². **Additional functions:** bus station, retail, administration. **Main materials:** steel, concrete, glass, bluestone paving. **Setting:** inner city.

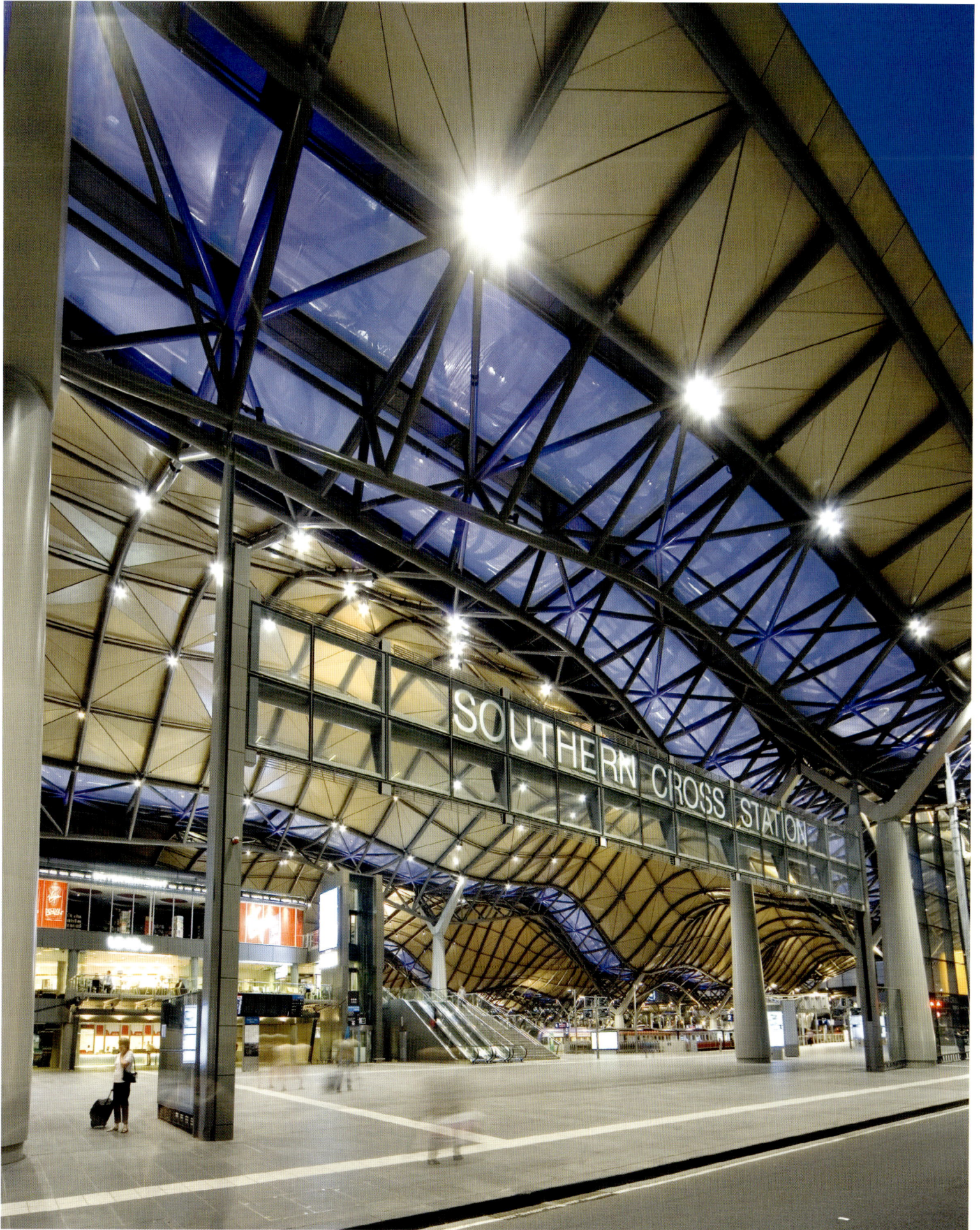

↑ | **View over platforms**
↙ | **Elevation**
→ | **Interior view,** escalators towards
platform level

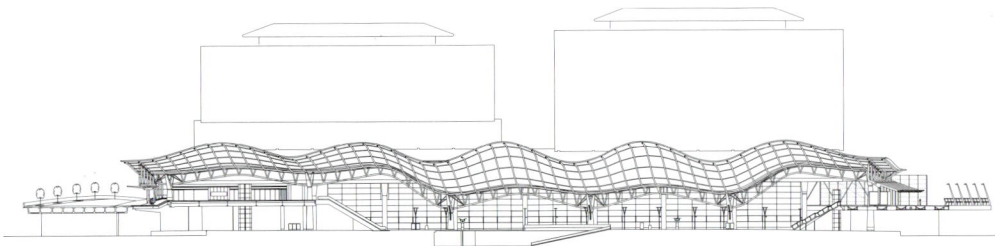

Makoto Sei Watanabe

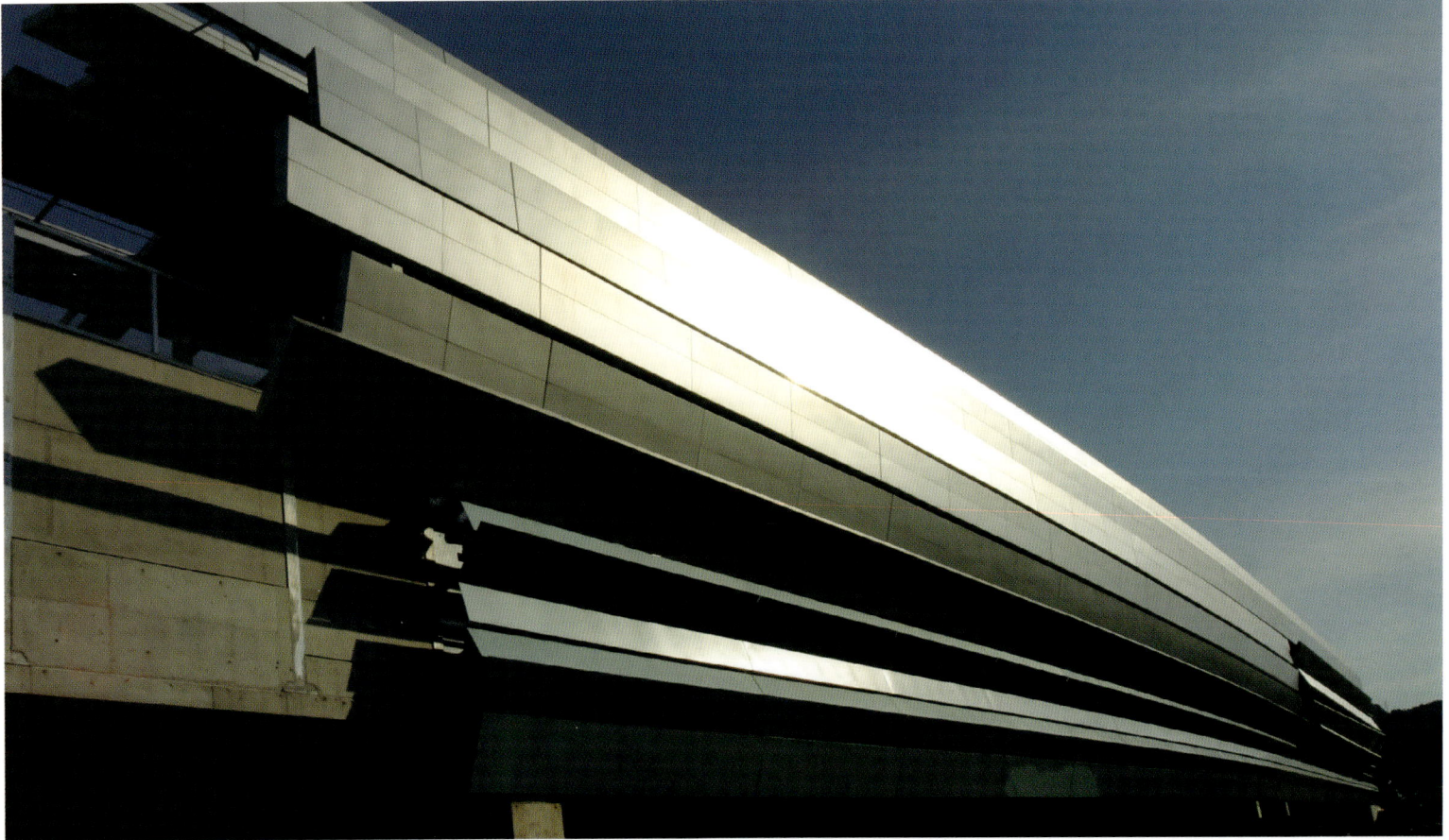

↑ | **Façade** composed of rectangular units

Shin-Minamata station
Minamata City

The roof, which simultaneously acts as the station's walls, consists of a collection of indiscriminate rectangular overlapping units. The design process began by imagining that a number of these units were gliding past and were suddenly made to freeze at a particular moment. The shape and state of the structure at this moment were examined to determine how much protection from rain and sun it could offer, whether sufficient wind circulation would be afforded and what degree of noise reduction from passing trains could be achieved. This method is related to induction design or algorithmic design, in which solutions to given conditions are found through self generation.

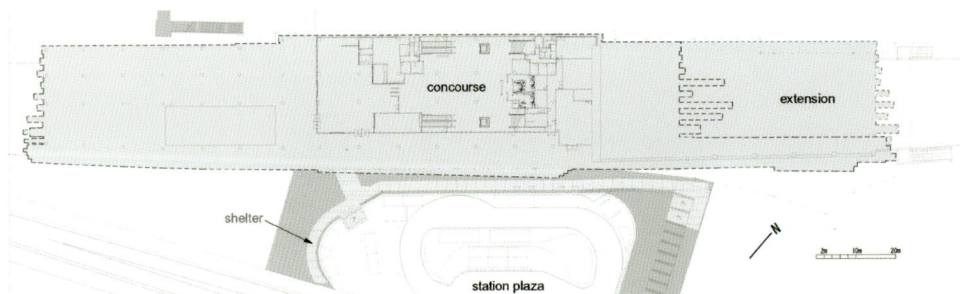

PROJECT FACTS

Address: Minamata city, Kumamoto, Japan. Cooperation partner: Seibukotukentiku. Train and sign design: Eiji Mitooka. Client: JRTT (Japan Railway Construction, Transport and Technology Agency). Completion: 2004. Type: heavy rail. Number of public levels: 2. Number of platforms: 3. Gross floor area: 4,867 m². Main materials: aluminum honeycomb core. Setting: urban.

↑ | **Platform,** with Shinkansen high-speed train
↙ | **Floor plan**

↓ | **Exterior view,** each unit piece was installed at a different angle

BDP – Building Design
Partnership Limited /
Peter Jenkins

↑ | **Main concourse**
→ | **Information screens** in main concourse

Chester station

Chester

The refurbishment and extension at Chester station has been progressing over the recent years. It is a very significant station of its time and belongs to the top sixth percentile of listed buildings in the United Kingdom. The new concourse structures aim to introduce contemporary forms which provide an organizing structure for additions, while treating original station principles with respect. This new approach envelopes the previous amendments, acting as an independent complement to the original forms. It was the designers' intention to create clearly modern additions articulated using historic fabric, in this case, pre-patinated copper.

PROJECT FACTS

Address: City Road, Chester, CH1 3NS, United Kingdom. **Client:** Arriva Trains Wales. **Original completion:** 1848. **Completion:** 2008. **Type:** heavy rail. **Number of public levels:** 1. **Number of platforms:** 7. **Number of passengers per day:** 10,500. **Gross floor area:** 6,100 m². **Additional functions:** offices, administration, staff facilities. **Main materials:** exterior: pre-patinated copper, glass; interior: birch faced plywood. **Setting:** urban.

← | Contrasting copper finishes

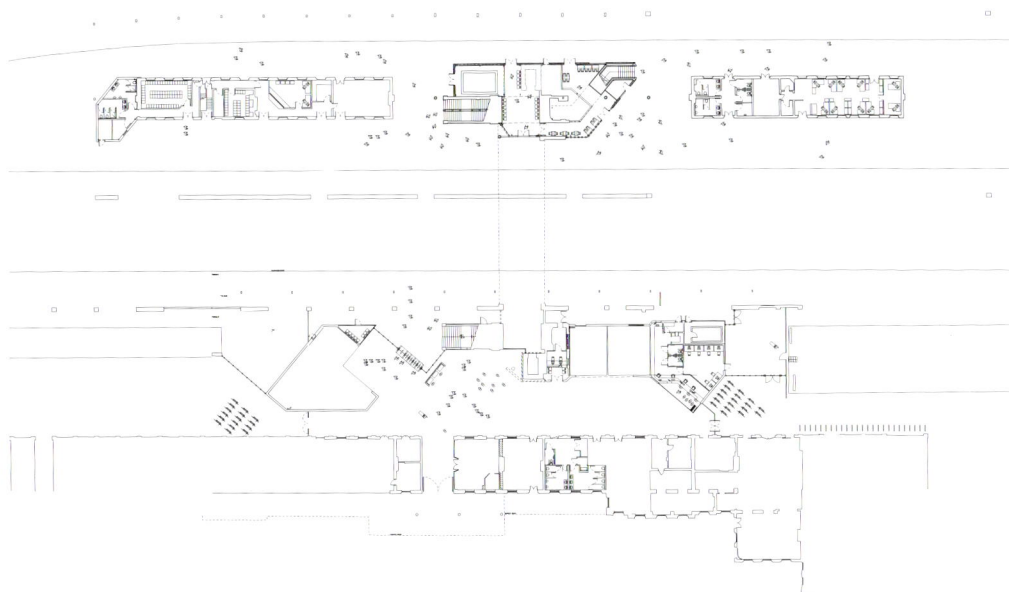

← | **Site plan**
↓ | **Ticket office,** clad in copper

Diamond and Schmitt
Architects

↑ | **View along the columns**
→ | **View of platform,** with TTC train

Museum subway station
Toronto

The innovative and dramatic design of the Museum station on the Toronto Transit Commission's University Subway Line re-imagines the station platform as a hypostyle Hall supported by archeologically inspired elements. The design of the five columns are based on artifacts from the Royal Ontario Museum and the Gardiner Museum, which are located above the station. The columns are repeated throughout the station's platform representing Canada's First Nations, Ancient Egypt, Mexico's Toltec culture, China's traditional culture and Ancient Greece. The new station design helps to orient subway riders to the city above, providing visual clues about the activities on street level. The project successfully combines functionality, aesthetics and culture.

PROJECT FACTS

Address: 75 Queen's Park, Toronto, ON M5S2C5, Canada. Client: Toronto Transit Commission. Completion: 2008. Original building: 1963. Type: heavy rail. Number of public levels: 1. Number of platforms: 1. Number of passengers per day: 8,500. Gross floor area: 2,700 m². Main materials: glass fibre reinforced concrete, aluminum panels. Setting: urban.

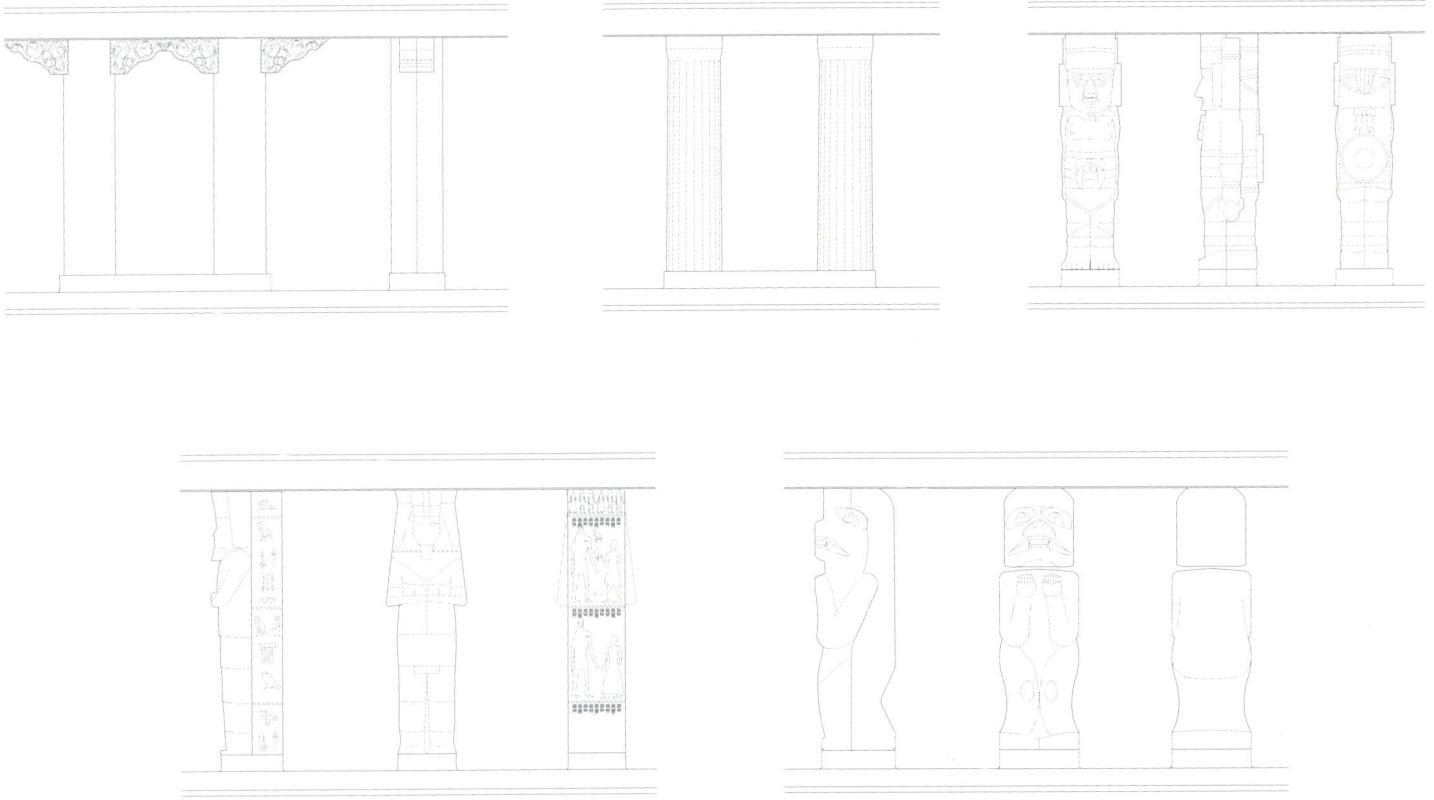

↑ | **Elevation,** for each individual column
← | **View of platform**

← | Toltec Warrior Column
↓ | Wuikinuxv First Nation Bear House Post

↑ | **Façade screen** with window slots
→ | **Façade detail**

TX / Kashiwanoha-Campus station

Kashiwa-shi

GRC units are made with molds. The design could use only a limited number of mold variations. In order to create diversity and prevent the limited number of variations from falling into monotonous repetition, simulations were carried out using recursive shapes that could be connected when reversed. A program 'Flow' /Induction Design was planned for this step. Rectangular segments of these sizes just happened to be cut out of enormous fluid surfaces that continue to expand forever. In this sense, there are rules which govern the birth of individual waves, but no rules that govern the whole. The whole is generated solely from the rules which produce the individual waves.

PROJECT FACTS

Address: Kashiwa-shi, Japan. **Client:** JRTT (Japan Railway Construction, Transport and Technology Agency). **Completion:** 2005. **Type:** heavy rail. **Number of platforms:** 2. **Gross floor area:** 3,748 m². **Main materials:** glass fiber reinforced concrete (3-dimensional). **Setting:** rural.

concourse   concourse

10   20   30

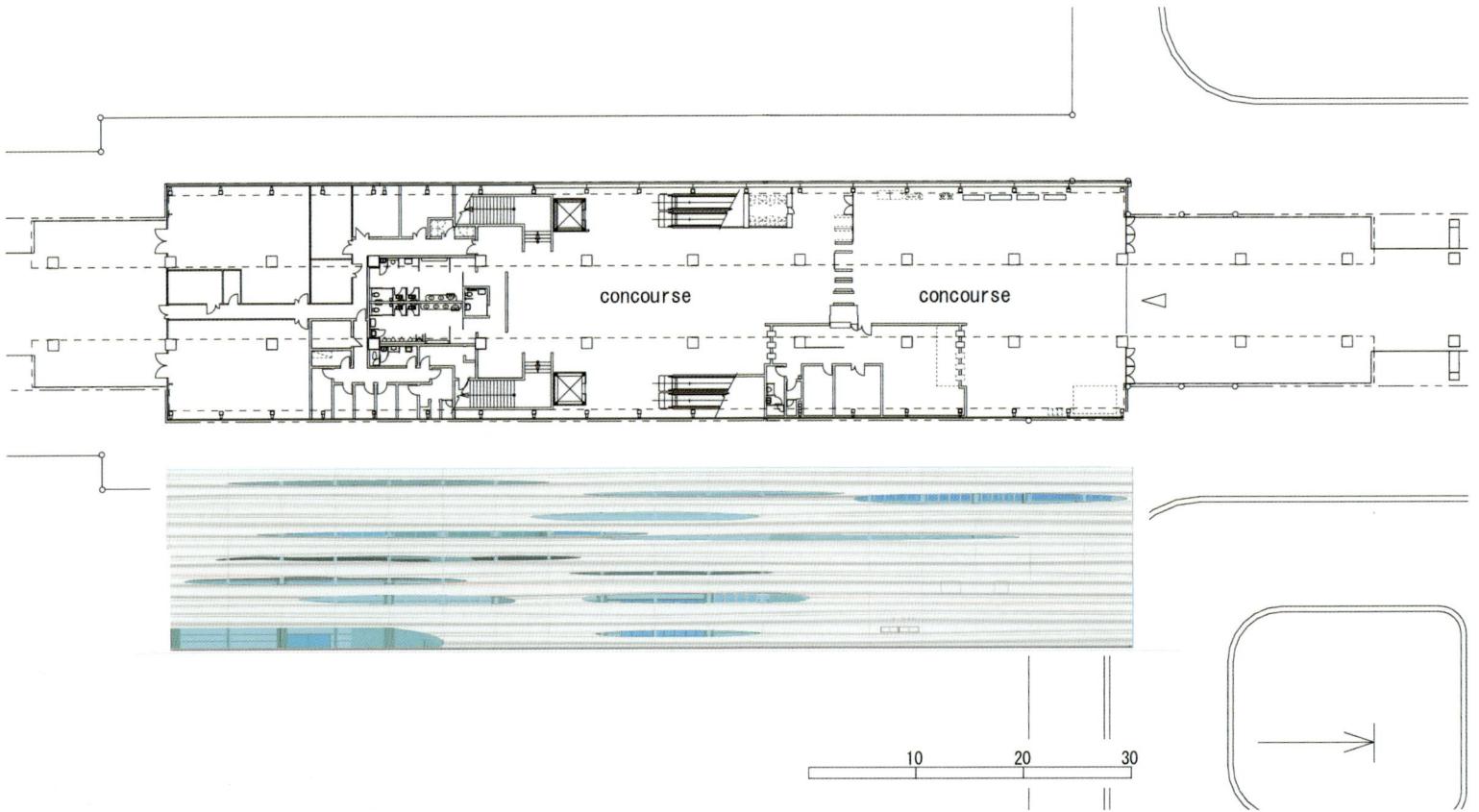

↑ | **Floor plan and elevation**
← | **Interior view**
↗ | **Façade skin,** in front of building wall
→ | **Perspective**

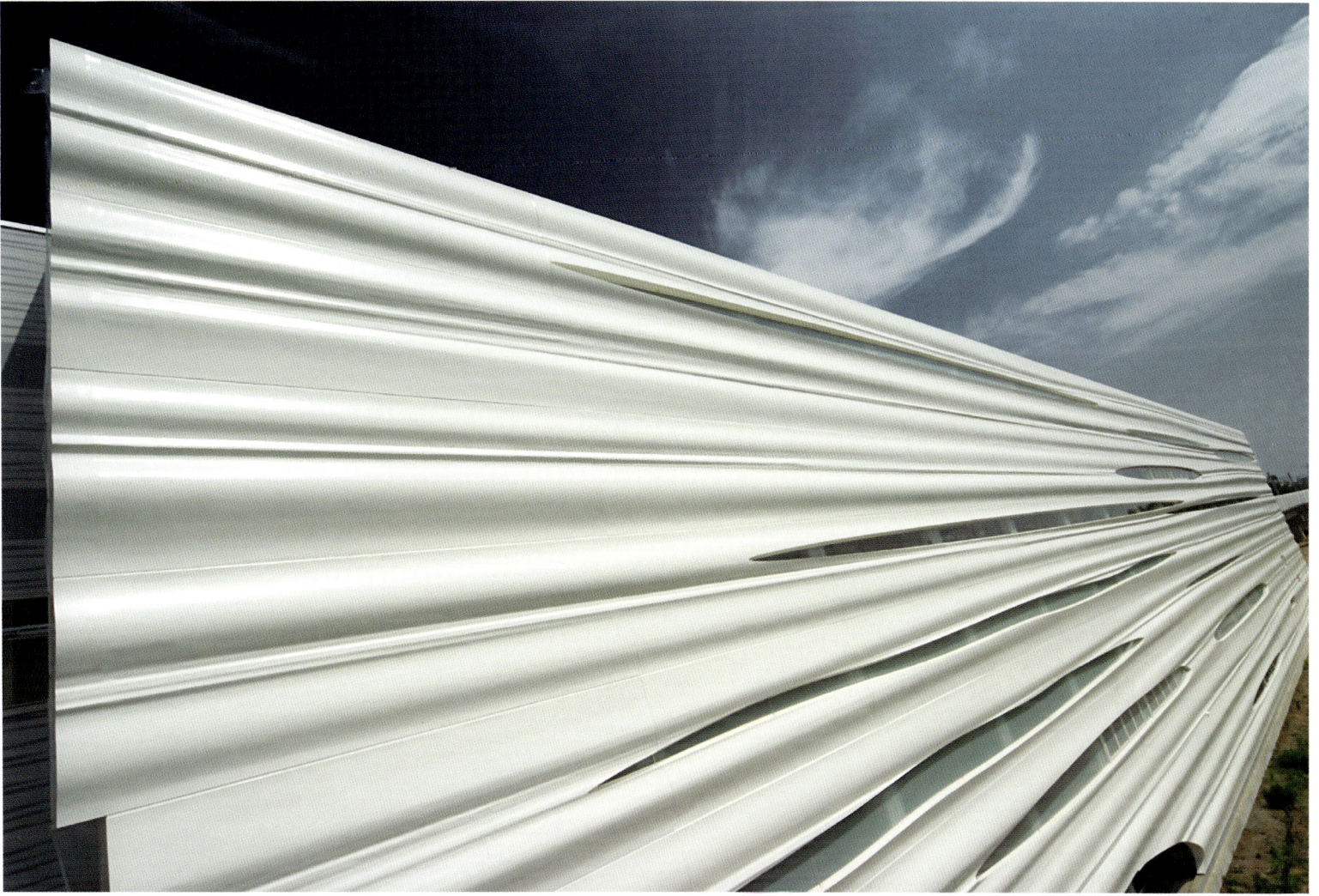

Santiago Calatrava
Architect & Engineer

↑ | **View of main concourse**
→ | **Entrance portal**

Guillemins TGV station

Lige

The city's existing station had to be replaced, because it did not fulfill the demands of high-speed rail travel. Calatrava's station design links a run-down urban area to the north and Cointe Hill, a less dense residential area to the south of the city, which were previously separated by the railroad tracks. Transparency is achieved by means of the monumental vault, constructed of glass and steel, which allows a sense of communication between the station and the city. Pedestrian bridges and a walkway under the tracks allow for fluid communication between the two sides of the station. Particular attention was paid to the architectural detailing of these transitional spaces.

PROJECT FACTS

Address: 4000 Lige, Belgium. **Client:** SNCB Holding, Infrabel, Euro Liège TGV. **Completion:** 2009. **Type:** heavy rail. **Number of public levels:** 3. **Number of platforms:** 5. **Gross floor area:** 49,000 m². **Additional functions:** transitional spaces. **Main materials:** concrete, steel, glass, blue limestone. **Setting:** urban.

↑ | **View towards main concourse,** through
structural ridges
← | **View over platforms**

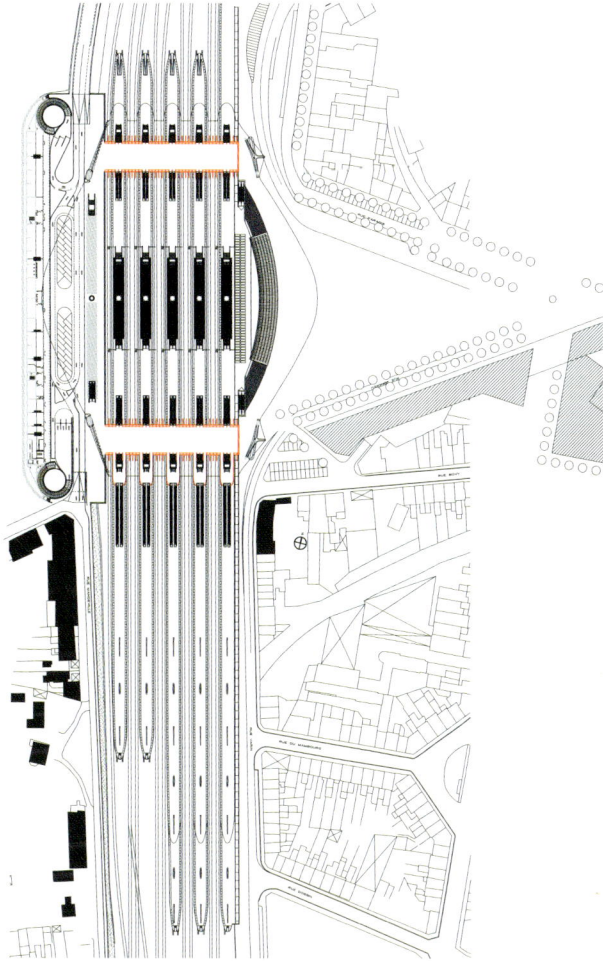

← | Situation
↓ | Perspective at dusk

smarch – Mathys & Stücheli
Architekten

↑ | **Bird's-eye view**
→ | **Detail,** stairways to the platforms

SBB passerelle "Wave of Berne"
Berne

On the one hand, the wave is a continuous fragment of the Berne train station, and on the other, it is an isolated building, which, as a specific "urban object" has the capacity to remold urban space. Thus it becomes an important factor in the perception of Berne due to its striking form. The wave creates a platform overpasses and canopies, which protrude from the main building, offering passengers the needed protection from the elements. The six platform canopies have different lengths, but optically display a uniform wave shape.

PROJECT FACTS

Address: Schanzenstrasse, 3011 Berne, Switzerland. **Planning partner:** smarch, Ostwald & Grunder Ingenieure, Conzett Bronzini Gartmann Ingenieure, Wild Ingenieure. **Client:** SBB – Schweizerische Bundesbahnen I-PM-OL. **Completion:** 2005. **Type:** heavy rail. **Number of public levels:** 2. **Number of platforms:** 12. **Number of passengers per day:** 50,000. **Main materials:** concrete, glass, wood, sheet metal. **Setting:** inner city.

↑ | **View along track**
← | **View upon platform**

← | South entrance
↓ | Cross section
↓↓ | Longitudinal section

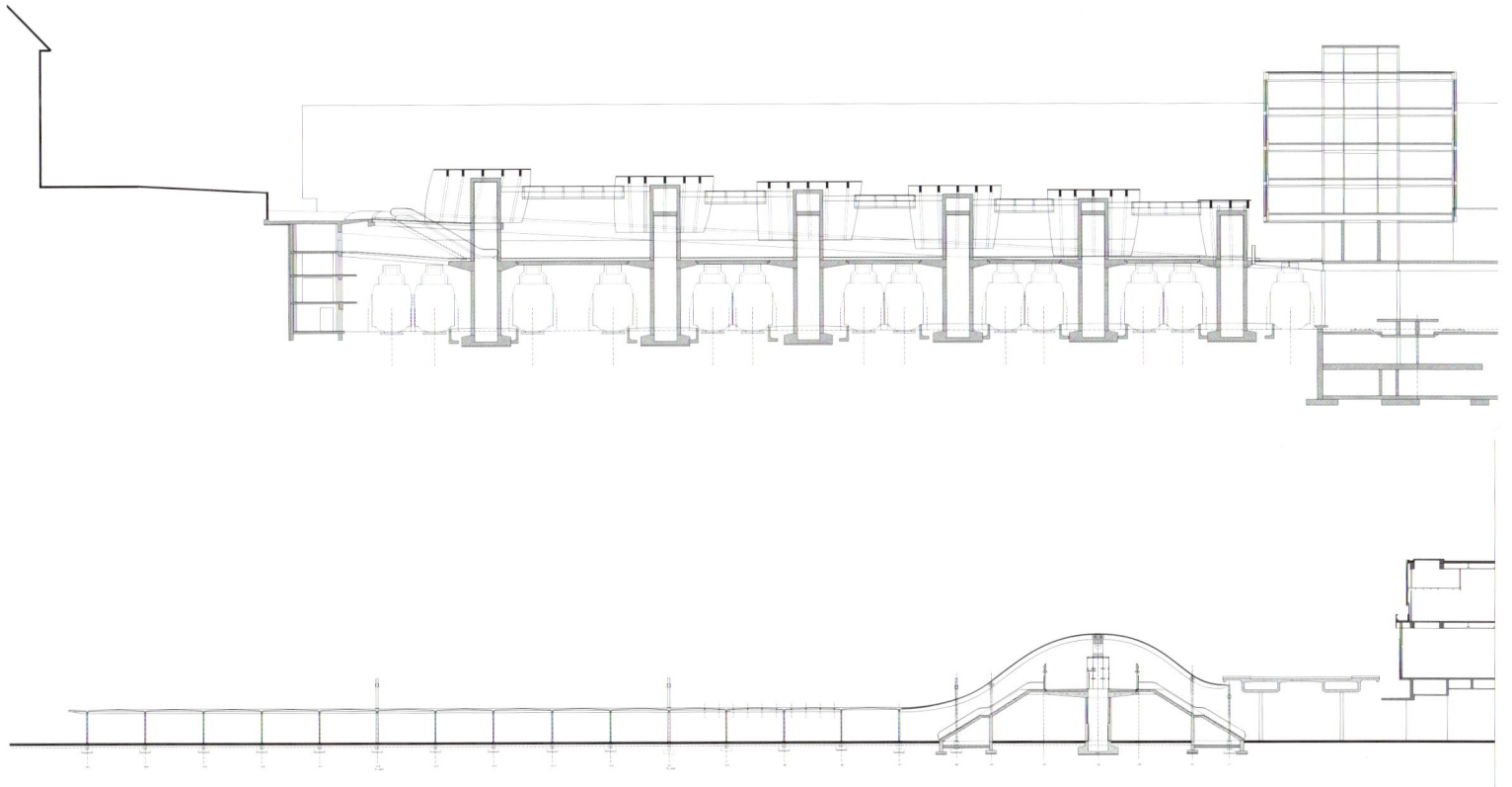

WOHA / Wong Mun Summ,
Richard Hassell

↑ | **Canyon view** from transfer level
→ | **View towards glass roof** from transfer level

Bras Basah mass rapid transit station

Singapore

The scheme sought to resolve the conflicting requirements of bringing daylight into a deep underground train station, and providing landscaping at the ground level. The solution was to provide a water-covered glass roof, which acts as both a reflection pool at ground level and a huge skylight. The design combines aesthetics and function to serve commuters as well as visitors. The skylight introduces light and vision deep into the ground, turning a potentially oppressive, labyrinthine experience into a clear, direct and exciting journey from the earth to the surface. The visual connection is also important for avoiding panic in a case of an emergency, for commuters will easily recognize how to leave the station.

PROJECT FACTS

Address: 65 Bras Basah Road, 189561 Singapore, Singapore. **Client:** Land Transport Authority, Singapore. **Completion:** 2008. **Type:** heavy rail. **Number of public levels:** 2. **Number of platforms:** 1. **Gross floor area:** 16,289 m². **Additional functions:** public square. **Main materials:** glass, steel, concrete. **Setting:** urban.

↑ | **Reflection pool,** covering the glass roof
← | **Pool** as forecourt to Singapore Art Museum

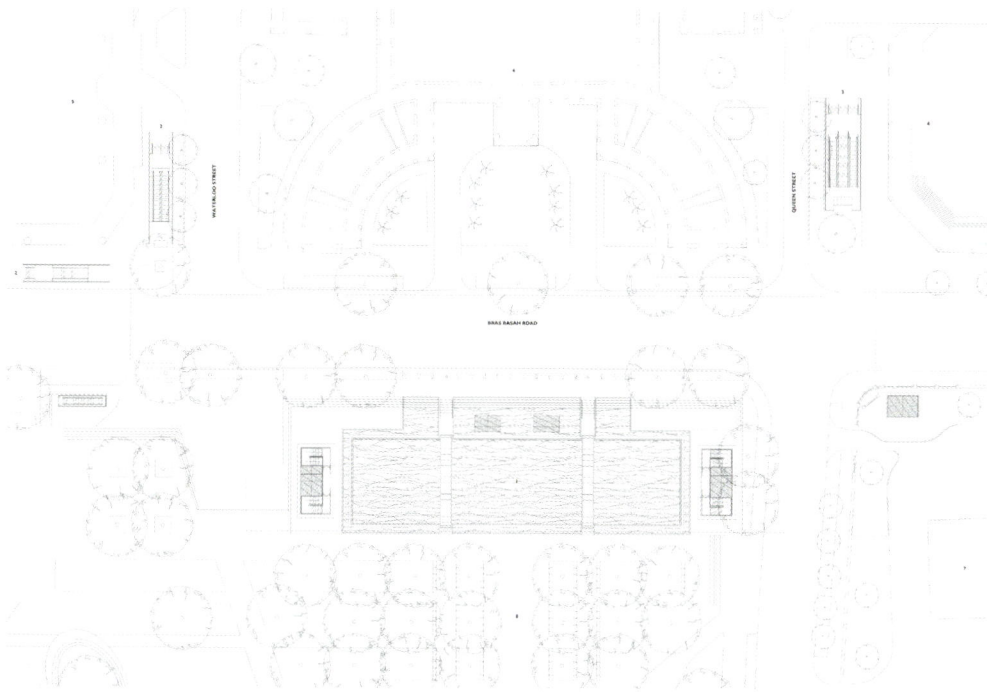

← | Site plan
↓ | Bird's-eye view

Chapman Taylor /
Simon Scott

↑ | **View of main concourse**
→ | **Seating area** at the platform level

St Pancras International

London

A new two-level concourse area with shops, cafés and bars was added to the 1868 Grade 1 listed building, accommodating 40 million passengers a year. The shops occupy the basement level, formerly a Victorian beer store, which opens up to the floor level above to bring in natural light and increased visibility. The design sensitively integrates high quality retail with the historic building fabric. The original exposed brick arches of the vaults are retained inside the shops to create a timeless design. Chapman Taylor also proposed the design standards for all commercial signs and retail fascia signs as part of the approvals that had to be obtained from the English Heritage and Camden Council.

PROJECT FACTS

Address: Pancras Road, London, NW1 2QP, United Kingdom. **Client:** London & Continental Stations & Property Ltd. **Completion:** 2007. **Type:** heavy rail. **Number of public levels:** 2. **Number of platforms:** 13. **Number of passengers per day:** 130,000. **Gross floor area:** 8,000 m². **Additional functions:** shopping mall, public space, parking facilities. **Main materials:** steel, glass, brick, concrete. **Setting:** urban.

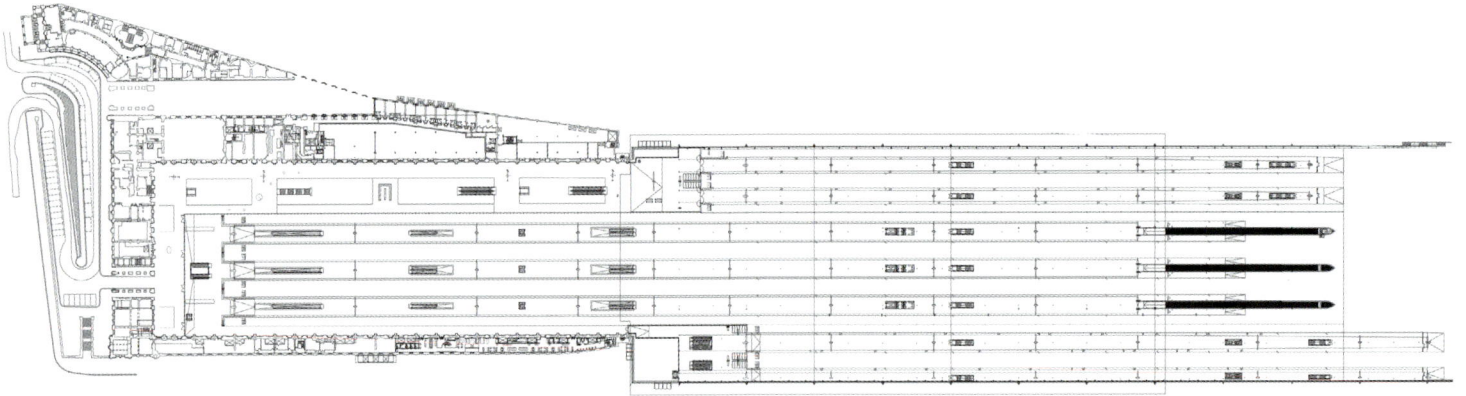

↑ | Site plan
← | Platform level

← | **Shopping mall**, detail view
↓ | **Shopping mall** in the restored lower level

↑ | **Exterior view,** in the evening sun
→ | **View from street level**

TX / Kashiwa-Tanaka station
Kashiwa-shi

The design aesthetically separates the street level from the upper levels, so that the functional aspects of different elevations don't influence each other. The uppermost level is covered by a flowing shape made up of a series of connected surfaces, some of which fold down to enclose parts of the concourse level. The shape varies along the longitudinal axis, resulting in a form with no two points having the same section. Rain gutters in the form of horizontal slits in the surface were inserted at several points due to the exterior being easily soiled by trails of rainwater. The resulting skin creates an illusion of being a huge frozen fluid mass that is cut with a knife.

PROJECT FACTS

Address: Kashiwa-shi, Japan. **Client:** JRTT (Japan Railway Construction, Transport and Technology Agency). **Completion:** 2005. **Type:** heavy rail. **Number of public levels:** 3. **Number of platforms:** 2. **Gross floor area:** 4,128 m². **Additional functions:** shops. **Main materials:** exterior: stainless steel; interior: cemented wood chip board. **Setting:** urban.

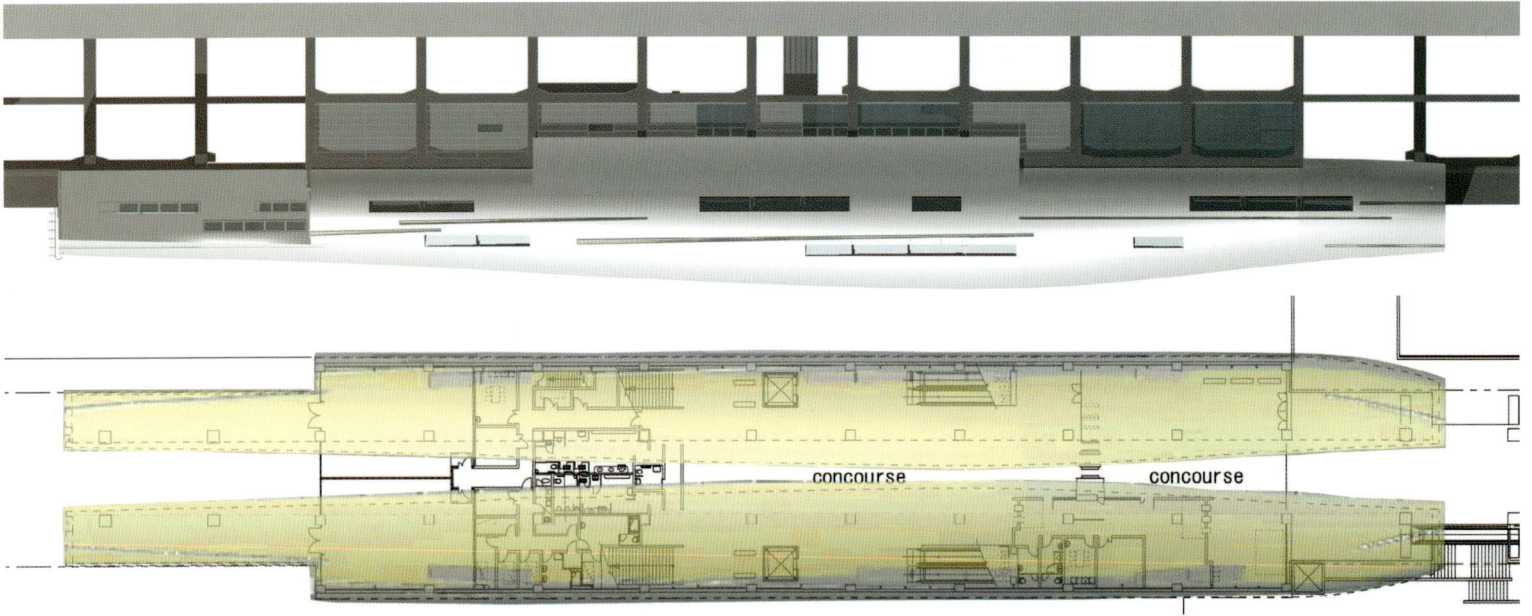

↑ | **Elevation and floor plan**
← | **Platform** and detail of handrail

← | Detail
↓ | Sketch

B&M architects Ltd. /
Jussi Murole, Daniel Bruun

↑ | **Staircase,** clad with perforated corrugated steel sheets
↗ | **New travel center,** with a bridge linking between Mikkeli center and the eastern suburbs
→ | **Pedestrian and bicycle bridge**

Mikkeli travel center
Mikkeli

Connecting the city center and the harbor, the travel center includes the old railway station, a bus terminal, freight terminal, harbor bridge, elevators, stairs and intermediate canopies. The bridge acts as an impetus for land development in the surrounding area. In addition to travel and parcel services, the freight terminal also has two commercial facility levels. Freight terminals, platform elevator towers and the piers are supported by an in situ-cast concrete structure. The curved, wood-clad mass of the freight terminal, the steel-structured bridge, canopies, stairs and facades are supplemented with perforated corrugated steel sheets, wood boarding and stair treads, and plywood ceilings.

PROJECT FACTS

Address: Mannerheimintie, Mikkeli, Finland. **Planning partners:** Juha Pajakoski, Ulla Kuitunen, Pasi Piironen (project team); Nordic interior, Heini Lehto (interior design). **Client:** City of Mikkeli, with Ministry of Transport and Communications and VR-group. **Completion:** 2007. **Type:** heavy rail. **Number of public levels:** 2. **Number of platforms:** 2. **Gross floor area:** 952 m². **Additional functions:** Mikkeli Occupational Health Department. **Main materials:** timber. **Setting:** urban.

↑ | **Goods station**
← | **Floor plan**, second floor

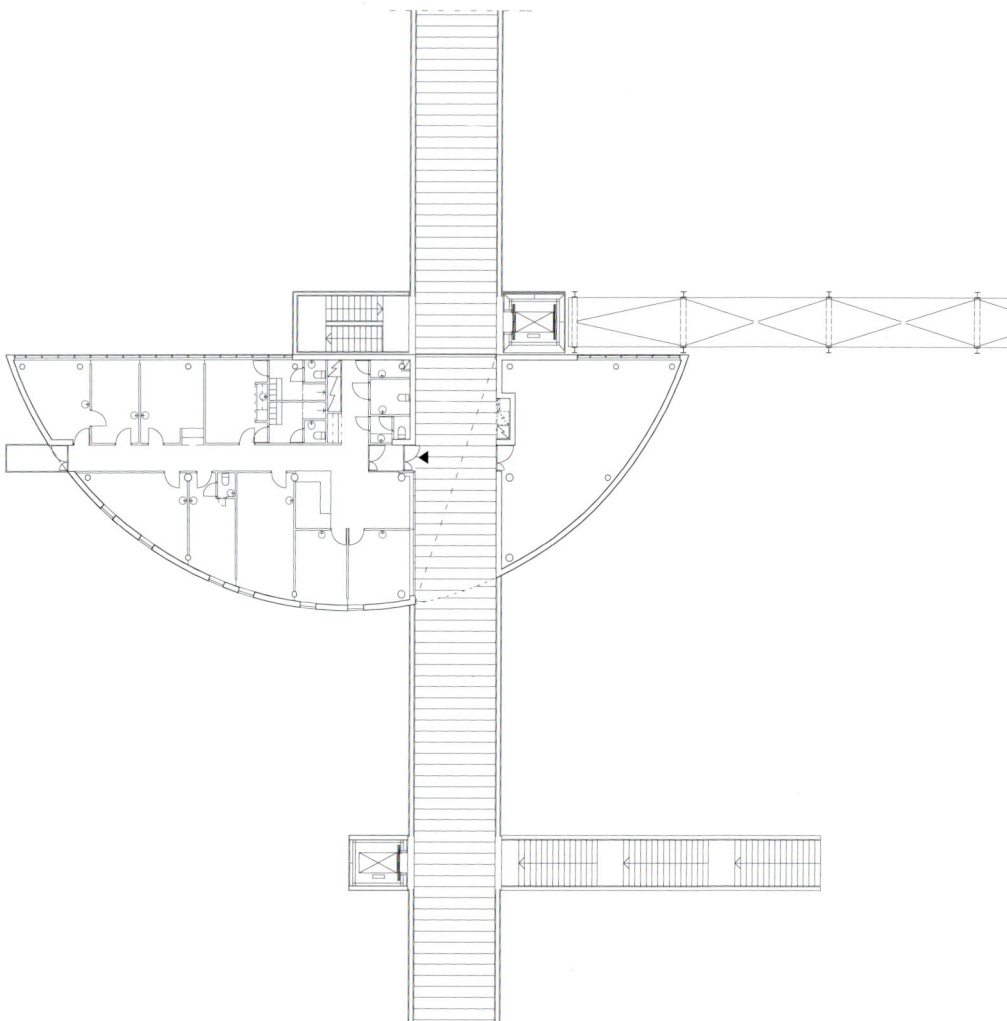

← | **Goods station,** curved façade
↓ | **Passerelle and platforms**

Aedas /
Alistair Branch

↑ | **Entrance area**
→ | **Platform level**

Rotherham central station

Rotherham

The existing station built in 1987 provides a key link to mainline services to Scotland, London, Birmingham and Manchester as well as other regions across the country. It is located on a constrained site west of the town center. The design of Branch new station sought to unify the station elements within a coherent architectural approach, using form and structure to create a dramatic and architecturally impressive gateway, enhancing the user experience. A new lightweight structure incorporating passenger facilities and staff accommodation replaced the existing building. Ramps were removed to both platforms and replaced by new enclosed stairs and lift towers to make the station fully accessible.

PROJECT FACTS

Address: Rotherham Central, Central Road, Rotherham, South Yorkshire, S60 1QH, United Kingdom. **Planning partner:** Arup, Leeds (engineering). **Client:** South Yorkshire Passenger Transport Executive, Yorkshire Forward, Rotherham MBC, Network Rail, Northern Rail. **Completion:** 2010. **Type:** heavy rail. **Number of public levels:** 2. **Number of platforms:** 2. **Number of passengers per day:** 1,200. **Gross floor area:** 1,150 m². **Main materials:** steel, brick, aluminum. **Setting:** urban.

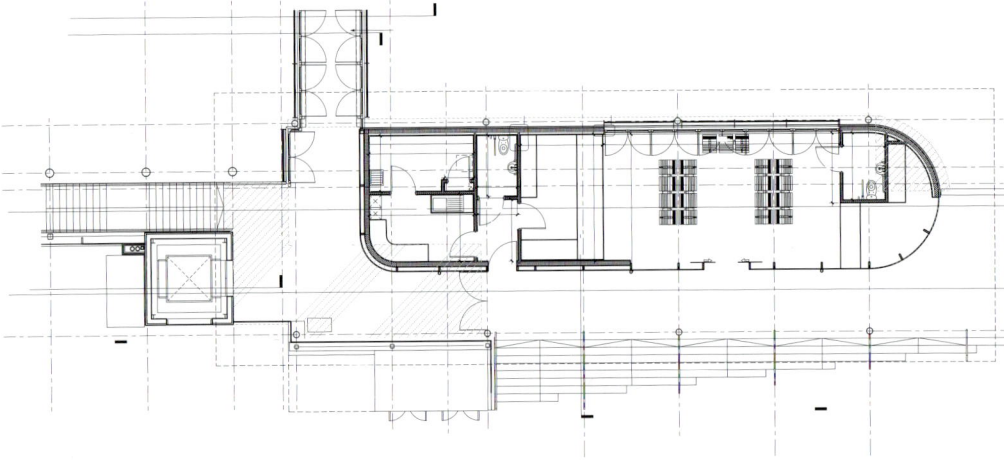

← | **Layout plan,** podium level
↓ | **Entrance area** at night
→ | **Aerial view**

Atelier 5
Architekten und Planer AG

↑ | Bird's-eye view
↘ | Sections

Head house building renovation Berne central station

Berne

The service center of the Berne central station was provided with a more attractive and clearly laid out design. The activities at the station around its main entrance that is open towards the city were organized with the help of the north hall, a vertical multi-level building. It provides illumination to the rear part of the station, accentuates the connection to the bus terminal, and accommodates new commercial uses. The interior of the location no longer resembles a cave but a casual sequence of rooms, substantially facilitating the orientation of passengers. Last, but not least, the replacement of the reception building façade, which was in need of renovation, significantly contributed to the new effect of the center.

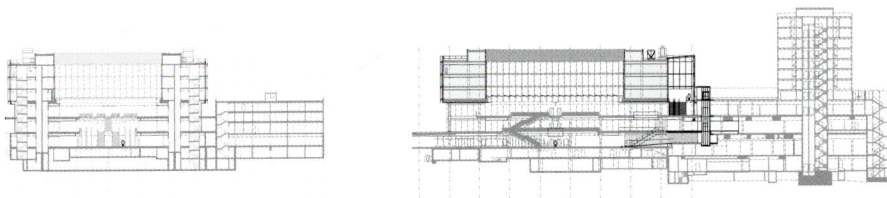

PROJECT FACTS

Address: Bahnhofplatz, 3011 Berne, Switzerland. **Planning partner:** Jauslin+Stebler AG, Caretta+Weidmann Baumanagement AG, KIWI Systemingenieure und Berater AG, Priska Meyer, Dipl. Architektin ETH/Lichtplanerin. **Client:** SBB Geschäftsbereich Immobilien. **Completion:** 2003. **Type:** heavy rail. **Number of public levels:** 3. **Number of platforms:** 17. **Number of passengers per day:** 150,000. **Gross floor area:** 33,137 m². **Main materials:** glass, steel. **Setting:** inner city.

↑ | **Glass façade** with station clock
↓ | **Transitional area**

↓ | **Pedestrian approach**

FAM Arquitectura y Urbanismo S.L. / Esaú Acosta, Raquel Buj, Pedro Colón de Carvajal, Mauro Gil-Fournier, Miguel Jaenicke

↑ | **Memorial at night** in front of the station main building
→ | **Passage way** with windows to memorial room

11th March memorial station
Madrid

The memorial was inaugurated three years after the terrorist attacks at their very site facing the train station building. It is an oval shaped glass cylinder that is 11 meters high and has a diameter of eight by 10.5 meters. The monument consists of two parts, the glass cylinder and an underground presentation room. Both parts are linked visually by a round window. The design creates the impression that the memorial, is a "shimmer of hope" rising up towards the city from the depth of the train station, the "site of sorrow". Inside the glass cylinder, spontaneous expressions of sorrow from citizens were engraved into a transparent plastic film.

PROJECT FACTS

Address: Av. Ciudad de Barcelona, Madrid, Spain. **Structural engineers:** SBP – Schlaich, Bergermann und Partner, Fhecor. **Client:** Madrid City Council and RENFE. **Completion:** 2007. **Type:** heavy rail. **Number of public levels:** 3. **Number of platforms:** 14. **Gross floor area of the monument:** 600 m². **Additional functions:** memorial. **Main materials:** glass, concrete, steel, ETFE. **Setting:** inner city.

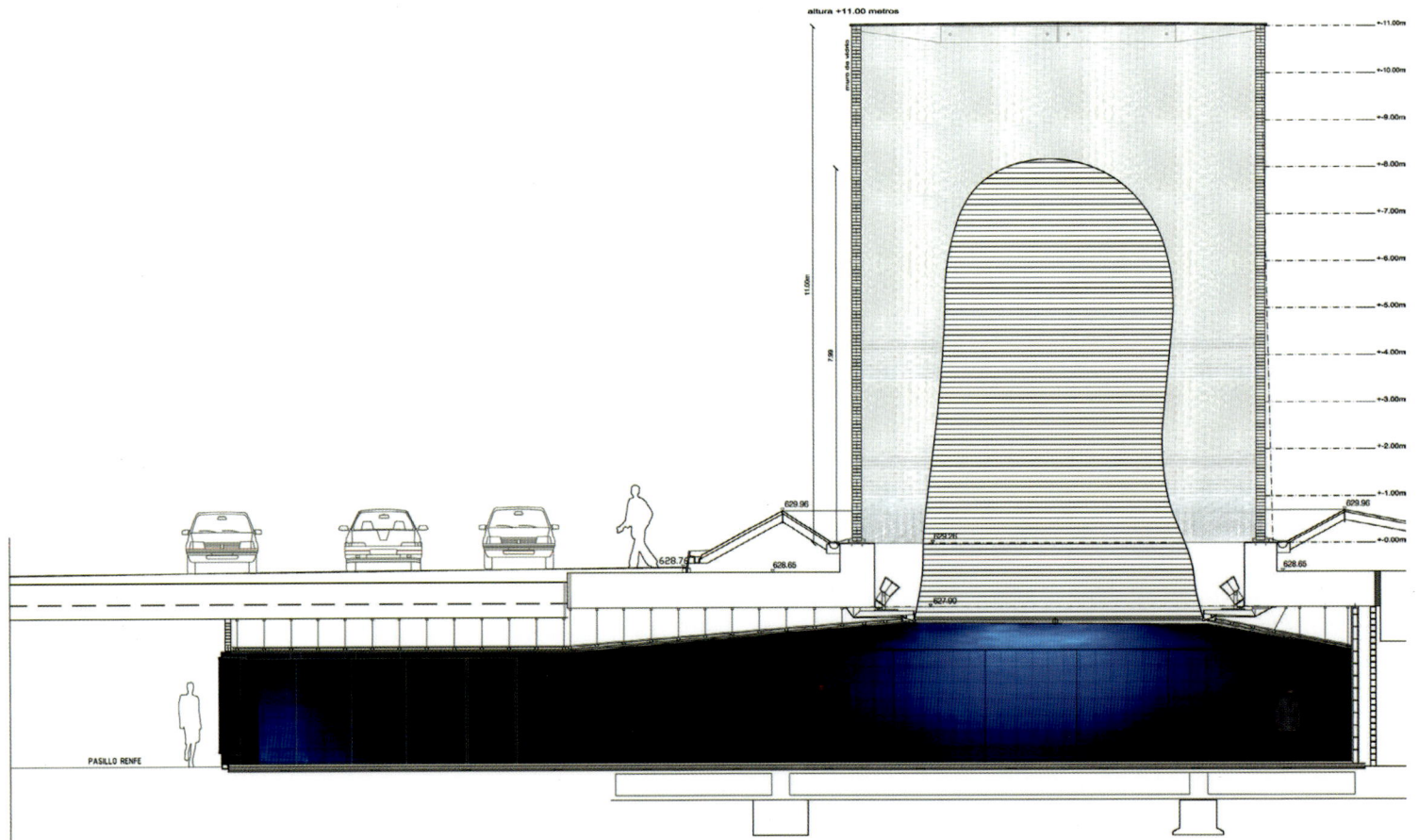

↑ | **Section**
↙ | **Plan**
→ | **Memorial room** with visitors looking up towards glass cylinder

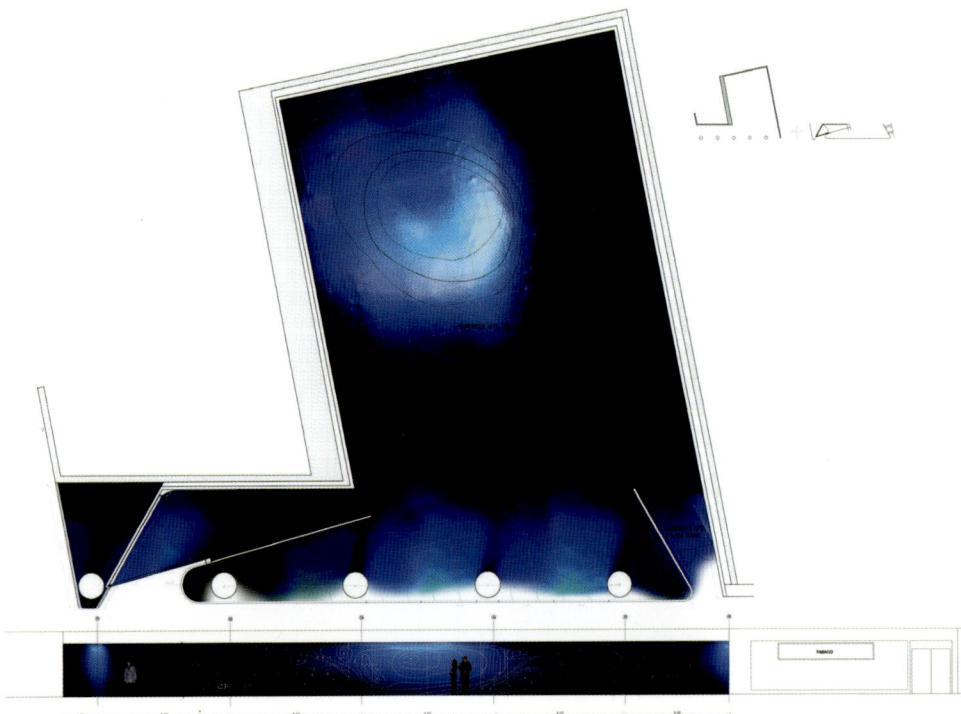

WOHA / Wong Mun Summ,
Richard Hassell

↑ | **Platform at basement,** with back-lit walls
→ | **Journey towards train platform**

Stadium mass rapid transit station

Singapore

The station is designed to enhance the urban quality of the surrounding areas with entertainment and leisure facilities. The open-ended building constitutes a strong element in the area, which future developments can be plugged into and organized around. To accommodate the large ground-level crowds, it has an at-grade, open-air concourse and plaza. A central skylight creates an attractive, day-lit platform. Openings in the elements above ground allow views down to the platform from the ground level plaza. The extrusion of the building's custom-designed ribbed aluminum cladding system can be arranged in four ways to create endless variations and different impressions of the relationship of the panels.

PROJECT FACTS **Address:** 3 Stadium Walk, Singapore 397692, Singapore. **Client:** Land Transport Authority, Singapore. **Completion:** 2008. **Type:** heavy rail. **Number of public levels:** 2. **Number of platforms:** 1. **Gross floor area:** 9,204 m². **Main materials:** aluminum extrusion. **Setting:** suburban.

↑ | **West entrance**
← | **Façade**

← | **Platform flooring**, reflecting the skylight
↓ | **Ground floor**, concourse level
↓↓ | **Sections**

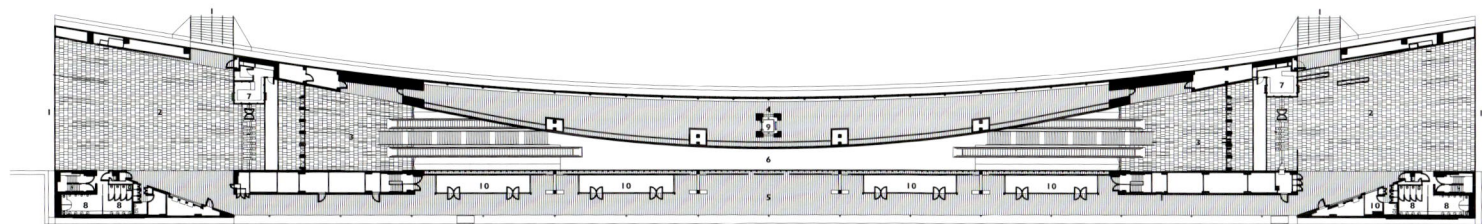

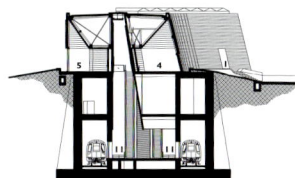

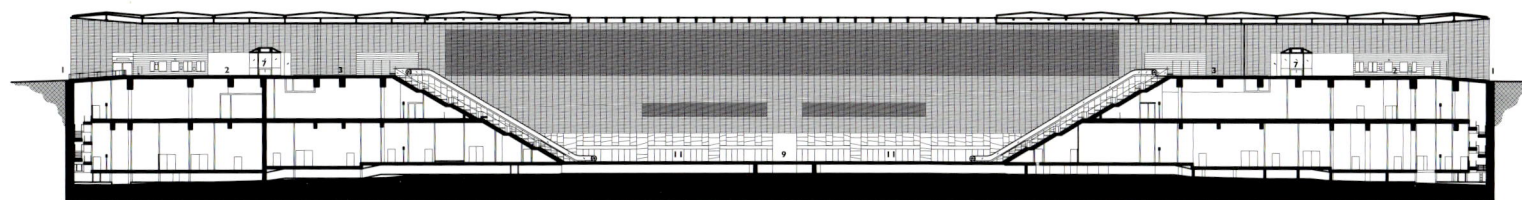

Santiago Calatrava
Architect & Engineer

↑ | **Sculptural form** of the central hall's superstructure

Airport station

Lyon

The dramatic form of the central hall's superstructure was derived from one of Calatrava's sculptures: a balanced shape resembling a bird at the point of flight. The glazed central hall, triangular in plan and spanning 394 feet, sweeps upward towards a service concourse on the east side, free of visual obstructions. The steel roof is composed of four converging arches with a curved, tapering spine. The arches to either side of the central concourse also form the portals of the platforms. A concrete vault of intersecting diagonal arches over the platforms creates a lamella roof spanning 174 feet. Above the tracks, the matrix of the roof opens to the sky.

Address: St. Exupery Aéroport, B.P 113, 69125 Lyon, France. **Client:** Rhone Alps Region and Lyon Chamber of Commerce and Industry. **Completion:** 1994. **Type:** heavy rail. **Number of public levels:** 2. **Number of platforms:** 4. **Main materials:** concrete, steel, glass. **Setting:** suburban.

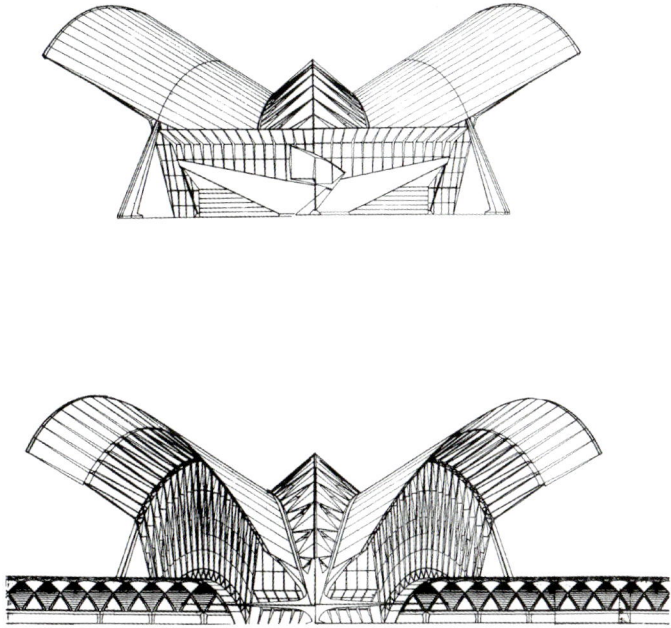

↑ | **Elevations**
↓ | **Lamella roof** over the platforms

↑ | **View towards lower level**

Light
Rail

↑ | **View along the track,** showing tubular
structure
→ | **Tubular structure** resting on V-shaped
columns

Station Beatrixkwartier

The Hague

The RandstadRail Station Beatrixkwartier is part of a larger project for a new urban light
rail network connecting the Hague and Rotterdam. The 400 meter-long viaduct running
along the Beatrixlaan consists of a supporting ring structure built using steel strips with
a diameter of about ten meters. These are interconnected by diagonally set tubes and
form an open tube structure. The tube's height makes it easy to bridge large spans. The
construction rests on V-shaped columns and provides room for two light rail tracks and a
platform between them. The 40 and 50-meter distances separating the spans necessitated
only few columns at street level.

PROJECT FACTS
Address: Prinses Beatrixlaan, 2595 BM, The Hague, The Netherlands. **Planning partner:** Gemeentewerken Rotterdam. **Client:** Projectorganisatie RandstadRail. **Completion:** 2006. **Type:** light rail. **Number of public levels:** 1. **Number of platforms:** 1. **Gross floor area:** 4,700 m². **Main materials:** steel, concrete, glass. **Setting:** urban.

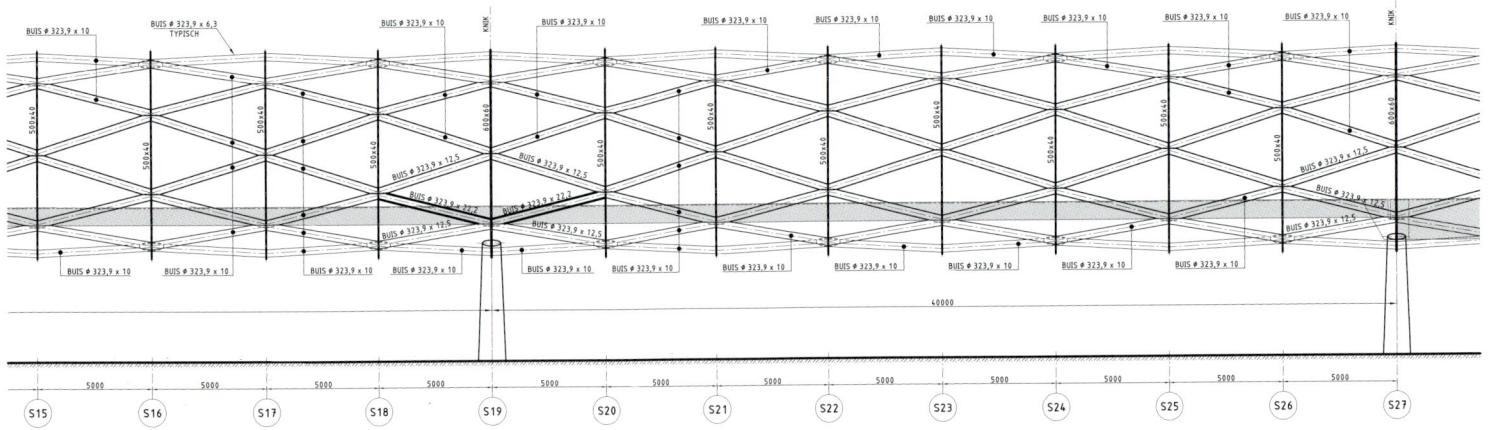

Longitudinal section / elevation labels:

BUIS ⌀ 323,9 x 10 · BUIS ⌀ 323,9 x 6,3 TYPISCH · BUIS ⌀ 323,9 x 10 · BUIS ⌀ 323,9 x 10 · KNIK · BUIS ⌀ 323,9 x 10 · BUIS ⌀ 323,9 x 10 · BUIS ⌀ 323,9 x 10 · BUIS ⌀ 323,9 x 10 · BUIS ⌀ 323,9 x 10 · BUIS ⌀ 323,9 x 10 · BUIS ⌀ 323,9 x 10 · KNIK

500x40 · 500x40 · 500x40 · 600x40 · 500x40 · 500x40 · 500x40 · 500x40 · 600x40

BUIS ⌀ 323,9 x 12,5 · BUIS ⌀ 323,9 x 12,5 · BUIS ⌀ 323,9 x 12,5 · BUIS ⌀ 323,9 x 12,5 · BUIS ⌀ 323,9 x 12,5 · BUIS ⌀ 323,9 x 12,5

BUIS ⌀ 323,9 x 10 · BUIS ⌀ 323,9 x 10 · BUIS ⌀ 323,9 x 10 · BUIS ⌀ 323,9 x 10 · BUIS ⌀ 323,9 x 10 · BUIS ⌀ 323,9 x 10 · BUIS ⌀ 323,9 x 10 · BUIS ⌀ 323,9 x 10 · BUIS ⌀ 323,9 x 10 · BUIS ⌀ 323,9 x 10 · BUIS ⌀ 323,9 x 10

40000

5000 · 5000 · 5000 · 5000 · 5000 · 5000 · 5000 · 5000 · 5000 · 5000 · 5000 · 5000

S15 · S16 · S17 · S18 · S19 · S20 · S21 · S22 · S23 · S24 · S25 · S26 · S27

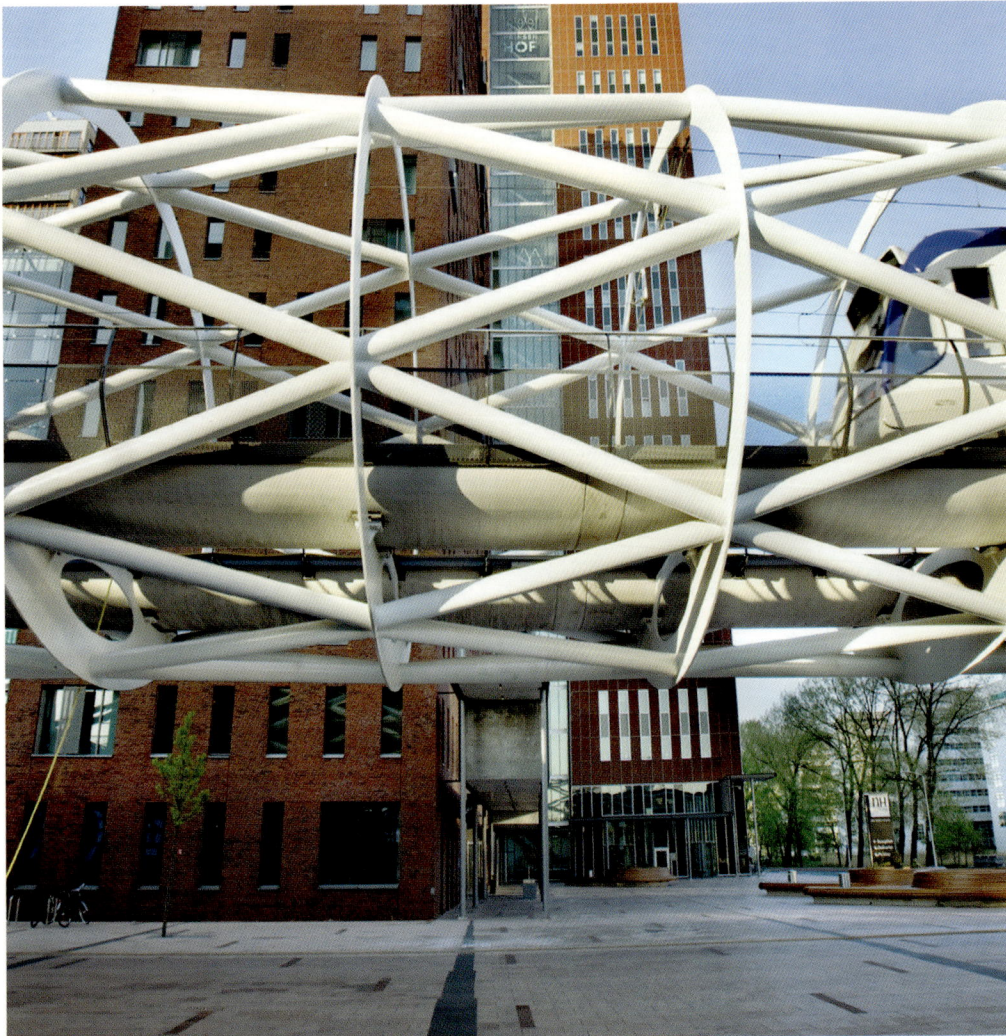

↑ | **Longitudinal section**
← | **Elevation**, open tube structure
↓ | **Cross section**

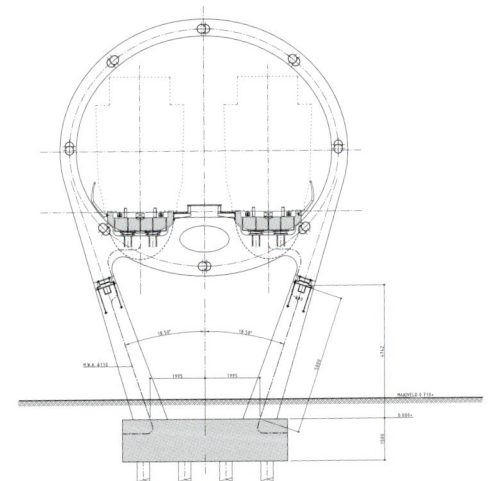

← | **Illuminated structure**, view from below
↓ | **Illuminated structure**, view from street

Foster + Partners

↑ | **Elevation**
→ | **View from the track**

Expo station

Singapore

Built to serve the new Singapore Expo Center, the design of this station is both a celebration of arrival and a response to one of the warmest climates parten the world. The station is announced externally by two highly sculptural roof elements which overlap to create a dynamic visual effect and appear to hover weightlessly above the heavy concrete base. A huge disc, clad in stainless steel, shelters the ticket hall and marks the station entrance, while a 130-meter-long, blade-like form, sheathed in titanium, covers the platforms, its reflective soffit constantly animated with the reflections of passengers and passing trains. The station's open form allows for a cooling flow of air to pass through the building.

PROJECT FACTS

Address: 21 Changi South Avenue 1, Singapore 486065, Singapore. **Co-architects:** CPG Consultants Pte. Ltd., PWD Consultants Singapore. **Consultants:** Arup, Davis Langdon and Seah, Land Transport Authority Singapore, Cicada Singapore, Claude Engle. **Client:** Land Transport Authority. **Completion:** 2000. **Type:** light rail. **Number of public levels:** 2. **Number of platforms:** 1. **Additional functions:** bus and taxi stations. **Main materials:** steel, concrete, aluminum. **Setting:** suburban.

←←| **The metal roof** providing a microclimate which is up to four degrees cooler than outside
↑ | **View from streetside**
↙ | **Cross section**

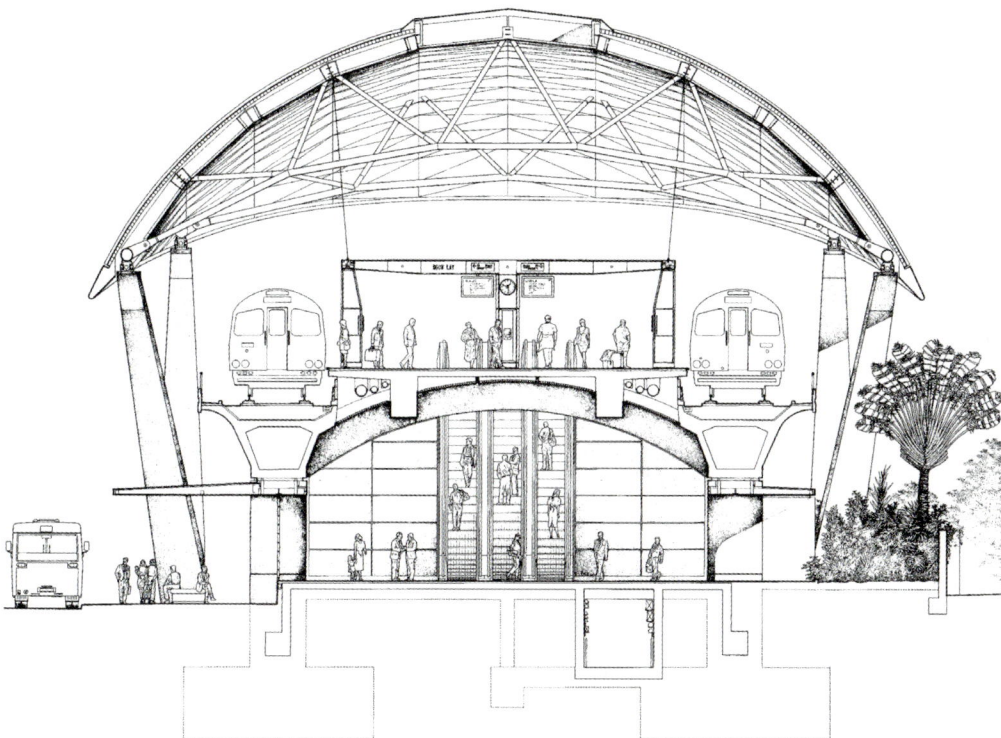

B&M architects Ltd. /
Jussi Murole, Daniel Bruun

↑ | **Bird's-eye view**
↓ | **Cross section**

Herttoniemi transport terminal
Helsinki

Situated five kilometers east of the Helsinki city center, next to East highway, Herttoniemi has been transformed from an industrial and harbor area to one of the biggest new housing developments in Helsinki. The Herttoniemi Center and transport terminal project, based on first prize-winning entry "synapsi", is an integral part of the new development in the surrounding area. It acts as a landmark and creates a frame for future multicultural city life. Herttoniemi Center is a dense urban multifunctional entity, incorporating a metro station, bus terminal, commercial center, offices, technical services, parking spaces and housing. The first part of the project, the technical service building for the metro line, will be realized in 2010.

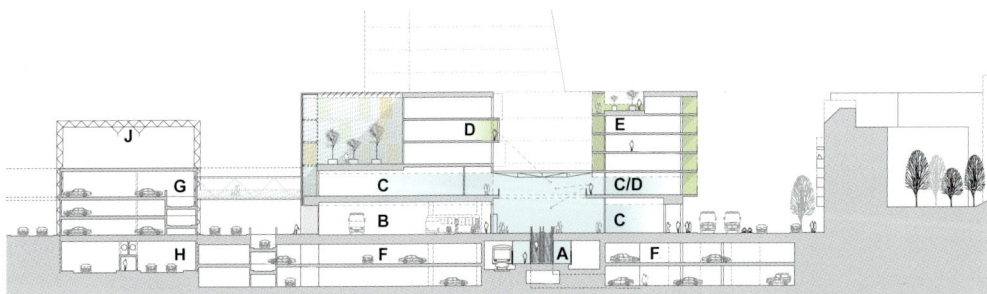

PROJECT FACTS **Address:** Herttoniemi, Helsinki, Finland. **Planning partners:** J-P Lehtinen, Matti Jääskö, Pekka Nurmi (project team). **Client:** City of Helsinki, City Planning Department. **Completion:** ongoing. **Type:** light rail. **Number of public levels:** 3–7. **Number of platforms:** metro: 12. **Gross floor area:** 55,000 m². **Additional functions:** commercial center, housing, offices, services, parking. **Main materials:** exterior: fiber cement, glass; interior: glass, metal. **Setting:** urban.

↑ | **Terminal hall** with office building in the background

↑ | **Conceptual illustration**
↓ | **Escalators in the terminal hall**

↑ | **Platform at dusk** with illuminated roof
→ | **Platform**

Metro station Heddernheim
Frankfurt / Main

Beginning to show its age, this station was rebuilt in the course of Frankfurt's metro network's expansion. In addition to elevation of platforms to train car level, the station had to be made visible as a homogenous space against the patchy structural massing around. Robust roof cubes with colorfully backlit expanded metal cladding were chosen as the means of creating a space of its own character in this inconsistent urban fabric. The clearly constructed, large-scale volumes architecturally reference the visual artist Donald Judd, who placed cubes within paintings and landscapes to create a space determining effect. The color and intensity of the backlight varies in response to approaching trains.

PROJECT FACTS
Address: Dillenburger Straße, 60439 Frankfurt, Germany. **Planning partner:** Bollinger und Grohmann Tragwerksplaner Frankfurt (structural engineers), Tools Frankfurt (light planning). **Client:** VGF Verkehrsgesellschaft Frankfurt/Main. **Completion:** 2005. **Type:** light rail. **Number of public levels:** 2. **Number of platforms:** 3. **Gross floor area:** 500 m². **Additional functions:** shop. **Main materials:** steel, fair faced concrete, metal mesh. **Setting:** inner city.

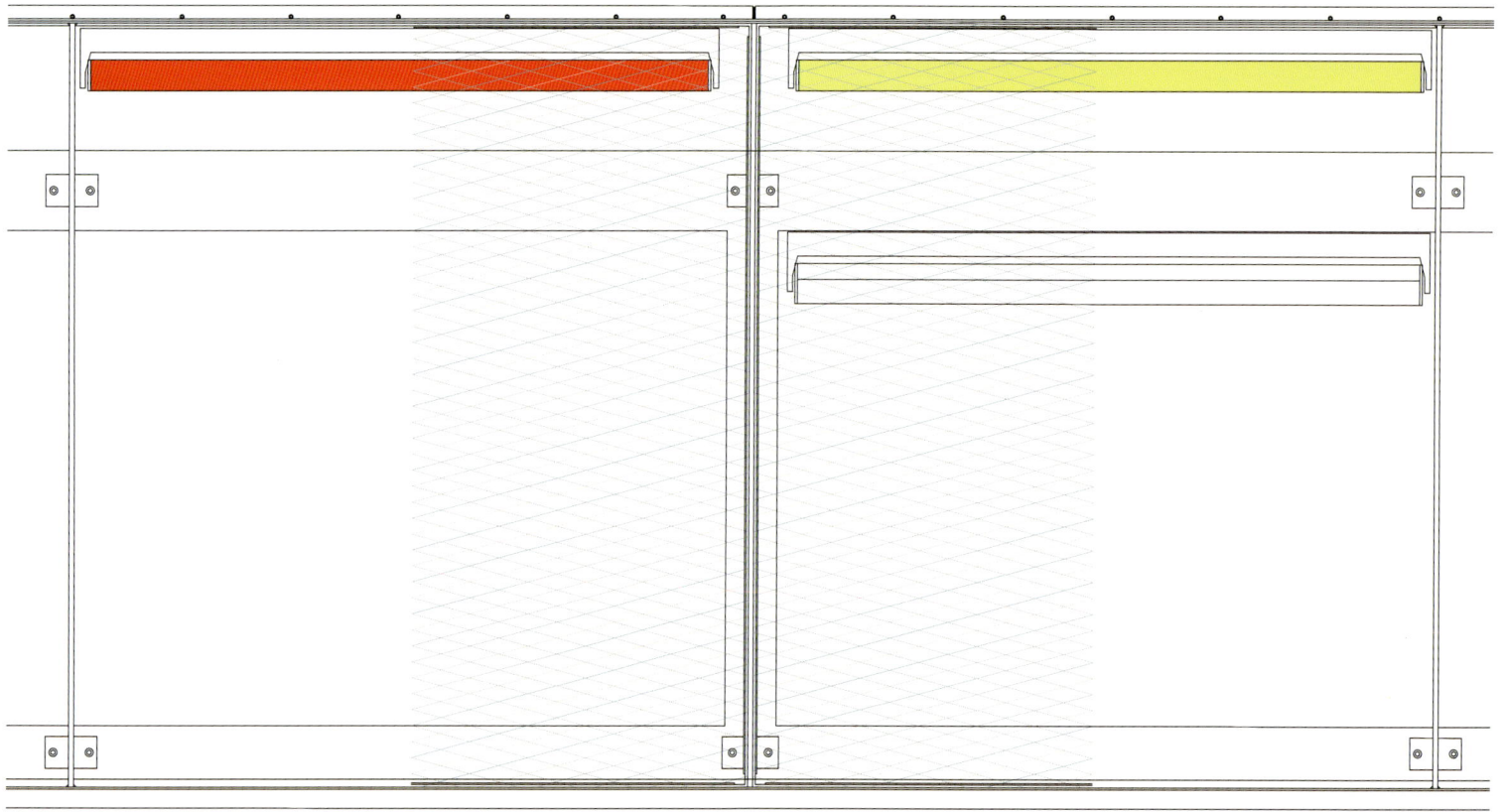

↑ | **Detail plan,** roof cladding and illumination
← | **Detail view,** roof cladding and illumination

← | **Station approach** at night
↙ | **Platforms at night**

Edward Suzuki Associates

↑ | **Aerial view,** the station connecting the
eastern and western part of town
→ | **Detail of promenade**

Saitama Shin-toshin station

Saitama

This station was designed as a gateway for the newly formed city of Saitama. In light of anticipation of several new distinctive facilities to be built immediately adjacent to the station, a seemingly shapeless structure resembling a flowing cloud was chosen in order to harmoniously blend into the context. To accommodate large numbers of travelers commuting to and from the adjacent sports and cultural arena, a 23-meter clear span of pedestrian deck promenade was integrated into the station's architecture. The resulting structure sports an elliptical roof over the promenade which continues in waves to cover the platforms. The roof is two-thirds steel and one-third glass, and allows sufficient daylight penetration.

PROJECT FACTS

Address: Saitama City, Saitama Prefecture, Japan. **Planning partner:** TIS Structural Engineers, JR East Japan Railway Tokyo Construction Co. (mechanical engineers). **Client:** Saitama Prefecture, JR East Japan Railway Co. **Completion:** 2000. **Type:** light rail. **Number of public levels:** 2. **Number of platforms:** 2. **Gross floor area:** 5,545 m². **Additional functions:** promenade. **Main materials:** steel. **Setting:** suburban.

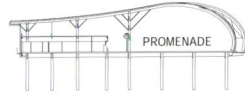

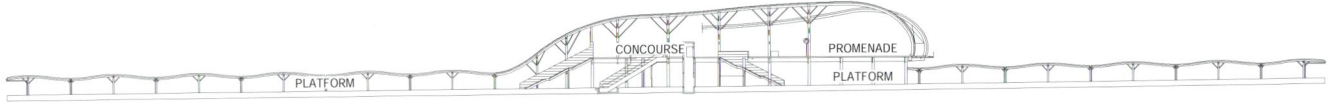

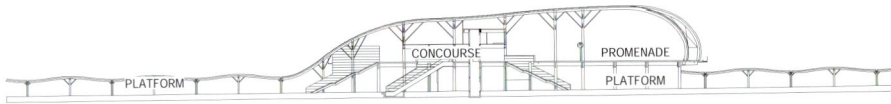

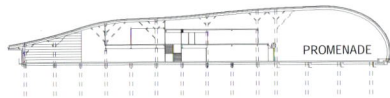

PROMENADE

PROMENADE

PLATFORM   CONCOURSE   PROMENADE
                                      PLATFORM

PLATFORM   CONCOURSE   PROMENADE
                                      PLATFORM

PROMENADE

↑ | Sections
← | **Bird's-eye view**, wave-like roof structure

← | **View of seating area** at the promenade
↓ | **Promenade,** east entrance

Pahl + Weber-Pahl
Planungsgesellschaft

↑ | **View from track**
↓ | **Longitudinal section**

Integration RegioTram
Kassel

Starting from 2007, RegioTram trains can approach the old Kassel main station from below in order to connect the intercity tram network with the Deutsche Bahn rail. This was made possible by a redesign of Kassel's old terminus station which, as a result, has experienced a revival. The design's idea is based on a single spatial form that shelters the RegioTram area with a support-free wooden shell and laterally connects to the train tunnel through using steel columns. This solution enabled the preservation of historic train platform roofs. Resting on steel supports without any tie rods, the wooden lamella roof shell became a unique eye-catcher to the Kassel traffic infrastructure.

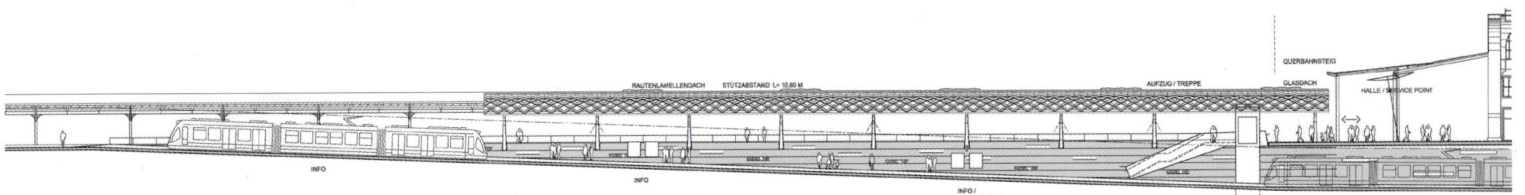

PROJECT FACTS

Address: Bahnhofsplatz 1, 34117 Kassel, Germany. **Planning partner:** OSD, FFM; Grossmann Bau, Rosenheim, et al. **Client:** KVC KVV Bau- und Verkehrsconsulting Kassel GmbH. **Completion:** 2007. **Type:** light rail. **Number of public levels:** 2. **Number of platforms:** 3. **Gross floor area:** 3,000 m². **Main materials:** glue-laminated timber, steel, concrete, glass. **Setting:** inner city.

↑ | **Wood structure of the shell**

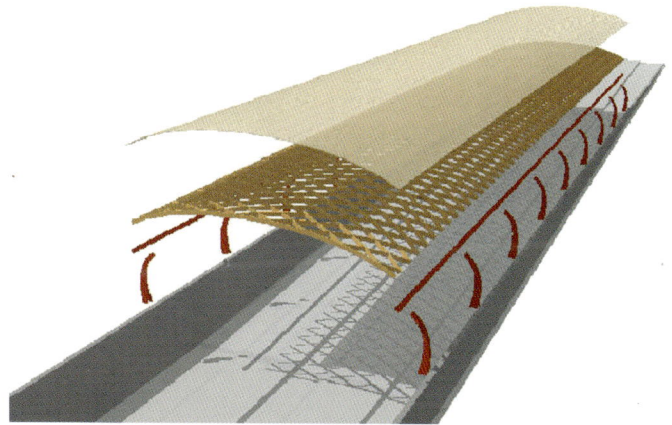

↑↑ | **Sketch** of the roof system
↑ | **Staircase,** view from below
↓ | **View from main concourse**

| Hans Moor Architects

↑ | **View of platform**
→ | **View from platform,** showing both public
levels of the station

Metro station Nesselande

Rotterdam

The Nesselande line is the latest extension of the Caland line, and will connect the new Nesselande suburb with the center of Rotterdam. The design of each station on this line will be executed by a different architect, and will attempt to integrate itself into the context of each station's specific site. The concept of the Nesselande station tries to cope with two opposing aspects of traveling: speed and continuity on the one hand, and interruption of these·properties on the other. The result is a station which offers generous space for parking and allows all passengers safe access during peak travel times. Additionally, the station was designed as a place for waiting, offering passengers a chance to enjoy the location should their journey be interrupted.

PROJECT FACTS

Address: Wollefoppeweg - Laan van dada, 3059 Rotterdam, The Netherlands. **Planning partner:** Gemeentewerken Rotterdam, ds+v Rotterdam. **Client:** RET Rotterdam. **Completion:** 2005. **Type:** light rail. **Number of public levels:** 2. **Number of platforms:** 2. **Number of passengers per day:** 3,500. **Gross floor area:** 1,800 m². **Main materials:** steel, glass, mozaic. **Setting:** suburban.

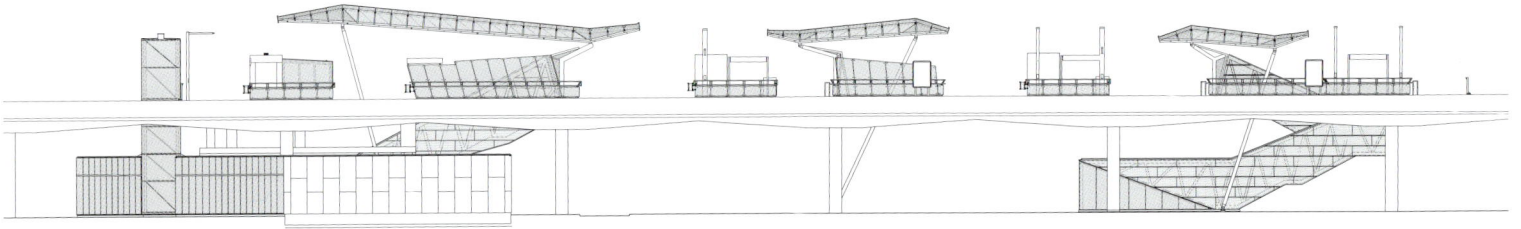

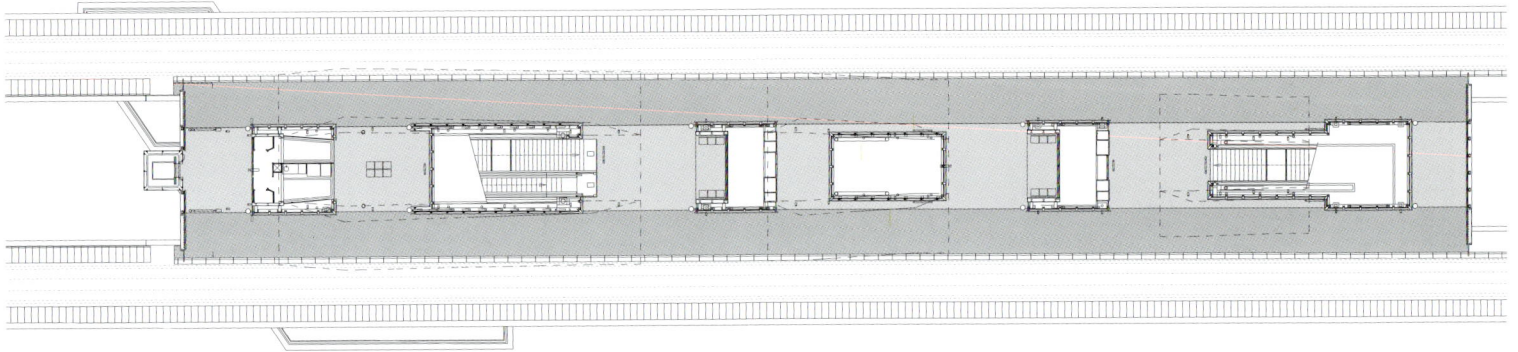

↑ | **Section and plan**
← | **View from ground level,** showing station and parking area at night

← | **View of station,** from below the rails
↓ | **Platform at night**

EM2N / Daniel Niggli,
Mathias Müller

↑ | **Two illuminated panels** establish a visual
and spatial relationship across the bridge
→ | **Entrance ramp,** a spatial part of the hall
was widened and charged programmatically

Station Hardbrücke upgrade
Zurich

The Hardbrücke train station received a new identity with the help of focused interventions, making passenger orientation inside easier. Additionally, the common area was made more pleasing to the eye. The station was anchored on two levels using large light panels, which act as double figures, visible from far away within the city fabric. At the level of heavily-trafficked Hardbrücke street, the panels create a visual relationship between the two bus stations located opposite each other. Below the bridge, the oversized illumination element guides pedestrians to the station entrance. Inner spaces have been structurally reorganized, receiving a clear visual appearance.

PROJECT FACTS **Address:** Bahnhof Hardbrücke, Hardstraße, 8005 Zurich, Switzerland. **Planning partner:** Jaeger Baumanagement, WGG Schnetzer Puskas Ingenieure, Vogt Lichtplanung, PGMM Schweiz, IBG Engineering, BAKUS Bauphysik. **Client:** City of Zurich. **Completion:** 2007. **Type:** light rail. **Number of public levels:** 2. **Number of platforms:** 4. **Additional functions:** underpass. **Main materials:** concrete, steel, glass. **Setting:** urban.

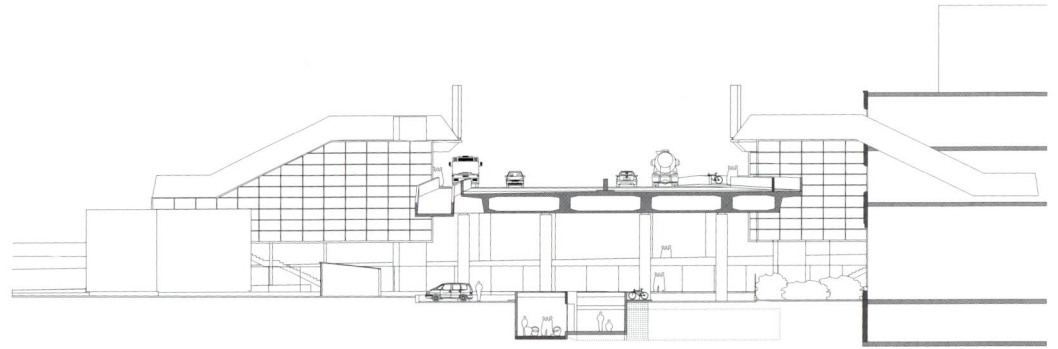

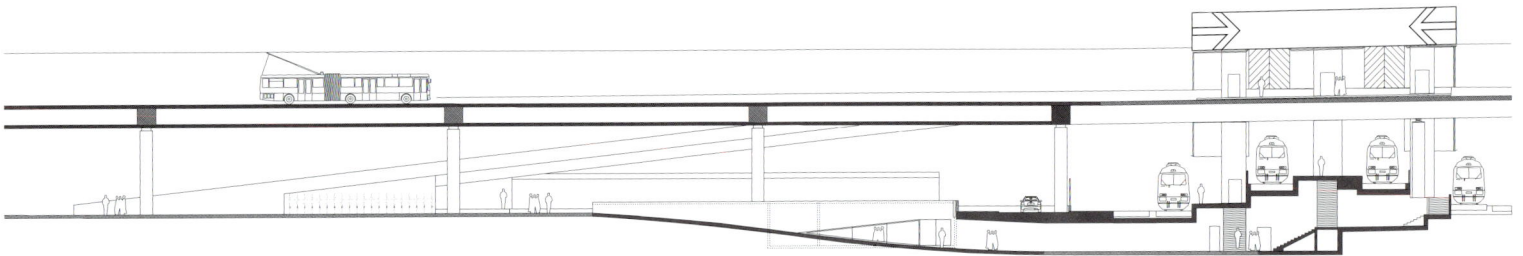

↑ | **Sections**
← | **Different levels visually connected** by
upgrading measures on and below the bridge

← | **View upon entrance ramp,** the soffit of the bridge is the roof of the station forecourt
↓ | **Entrance to the "square-hall"** is marked by an illuminated panel

Ateliers Jean Nouvel

↑ | **Pincetto station,** view from platform
→ | **Pincetto station,** different materials and
lights

Minimetro

Perugia

By introducing the new Minimetro the city hopes to relieve the pressure of individual transport on the city center. It consists of 25 driverless cabins with a capacity of 25 passengers on a circular track serving the western periphery of the city with the center on a length of three kilometers with two main stations and five way stations in 60-second cycles. Nouvel was responsible for both the design of the stations as well as the "linea rossa". He combined a modern architectural style suitable to the innovative power of the new transportation mode with a sensitive integration of the line into the hilly landscape and the historic setting.

PROJECT FACTS Address: Perugia, Italy. **Planning partner:** Studio Ciuffini / NAIF. **Client:** City of Perugia. **Completion:** 2008. **Type:** light rail. **Number of public levels:** different numbers. **Number of platforms:** 2 each station. **Number of passengers:** 8,000 passengers per hour. **Main materials:** concrete, stone, stainless steel. **Setting:** suburban and urban.

↑ | **Cortonese station,** reflection on the roof
← | **Route beneath the city**
↙ | **Massiano station** with different paths

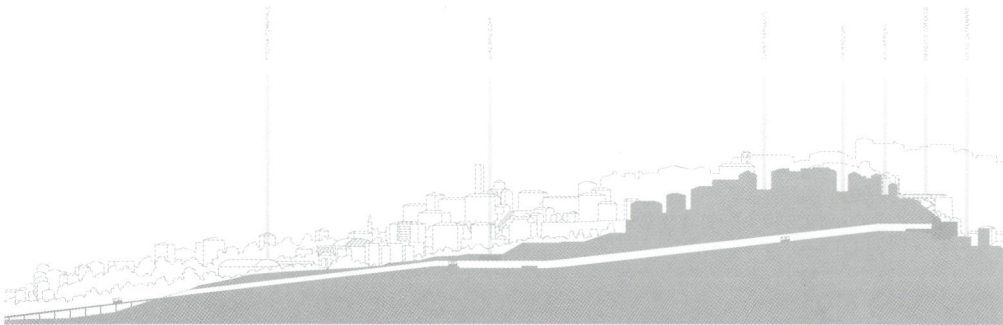

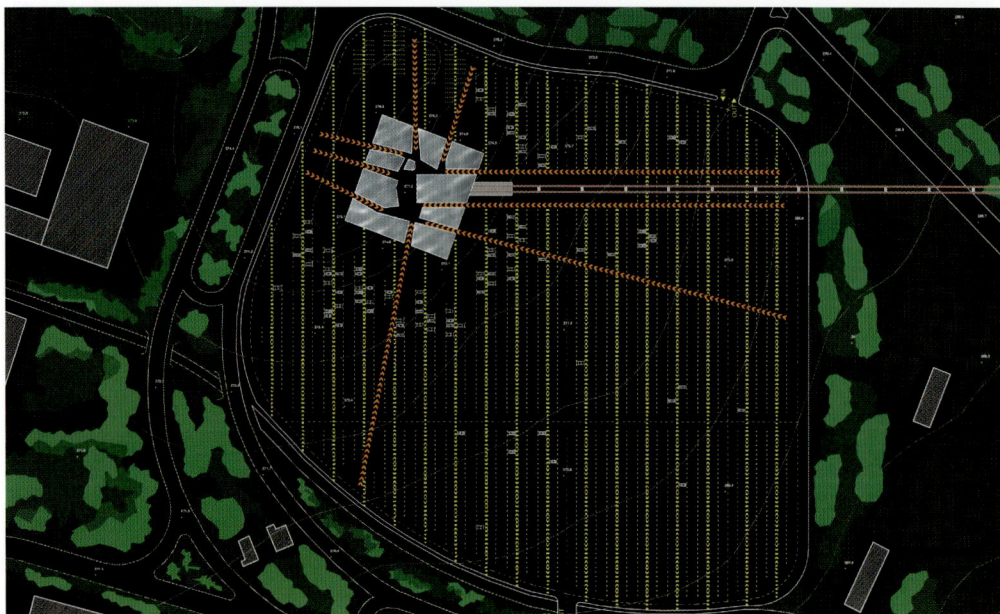

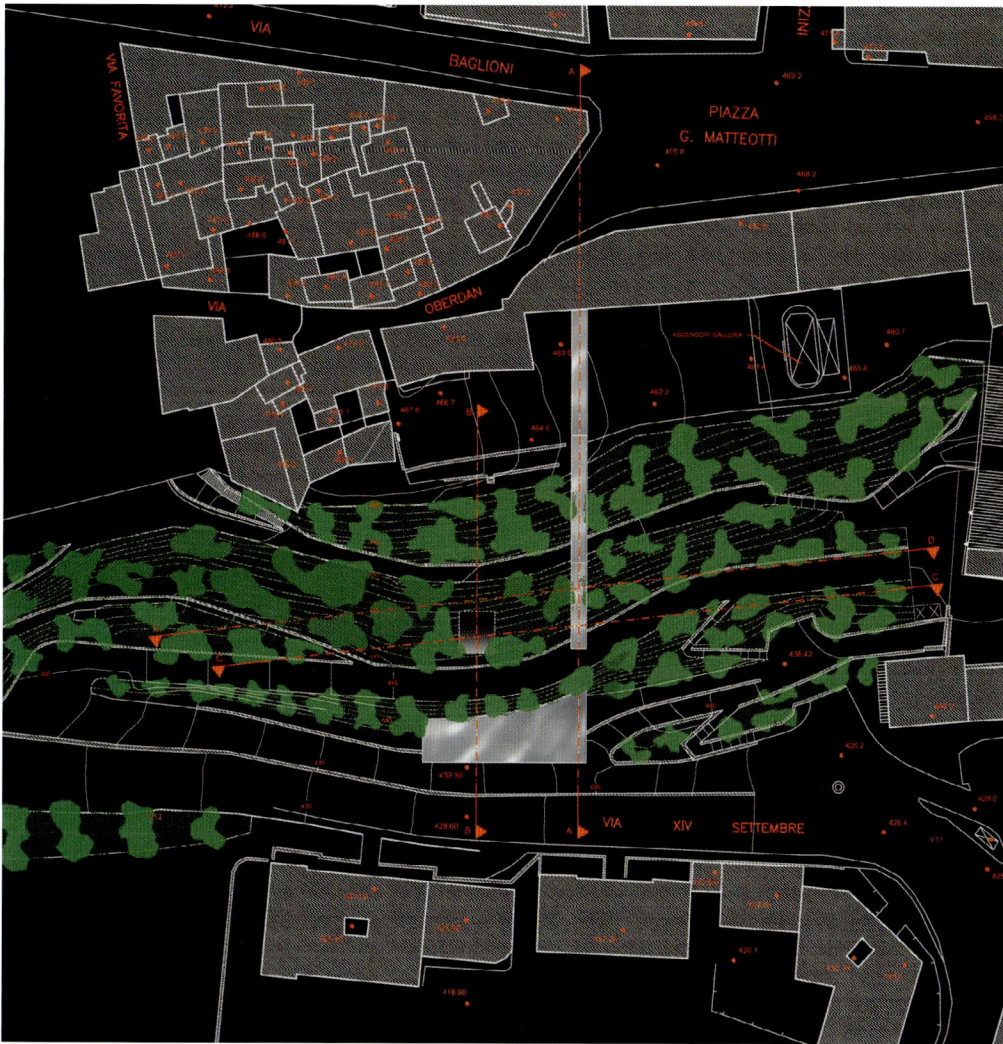

← | **Pincetto station** at a hillsite
↓ | **Open station rendering**

Busby Perkins+Will
Architects Co.

↑ | **View from street level,** station hovering nine meters above the highway
→ | **Aerial view** at night

Brentwood town center station

Burnaby

This station is the jewel of Metro Vancouver's rapid transit Millennium Line. Because of its flagship location, it was vital that Brentwood be particulary unique and enticing. Hovering nine meters above the highway, the station provides a sleek, high-tech aesthetic for the Skytrain line. It comprises two distinct volumes: A streamlined platform lightly touches down on a broad mezzanine. The mezzanine spans the highway and creates an open public space, while the platform enclosure functions as a beacon. A single mass-produced glass panel, mounted on rotating brackets, is used for the entire glazing system, which is supported by curved steel and wood ribs of varying size and height.

PROJECT FACTS

Address: 4533 Lougheed Highway, Burnaby, BC V5B2Z6, Canada. **Client:** Rapid Transit Project Office. **Completion:** 2002. **Type:** light rail. **Number of public levels:** 2. **Number of platforms:** 2. **Number of passengers per day:** 59,100. **Gross floor area:** 2,100 m². **Main materials:** exterior: concrete, glass, steel; interior: wood, glass, steel. **Setting:** suburban.

↑ | **View of platform,** curved ceiling structure clad in wood
← | **View of structural ribs** of wood and steel
↓ | **Plan of structural rib**

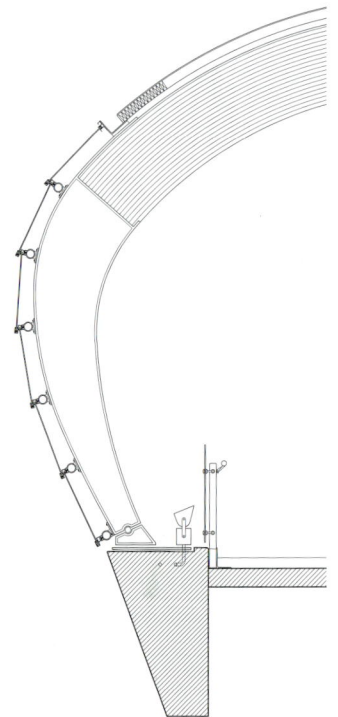

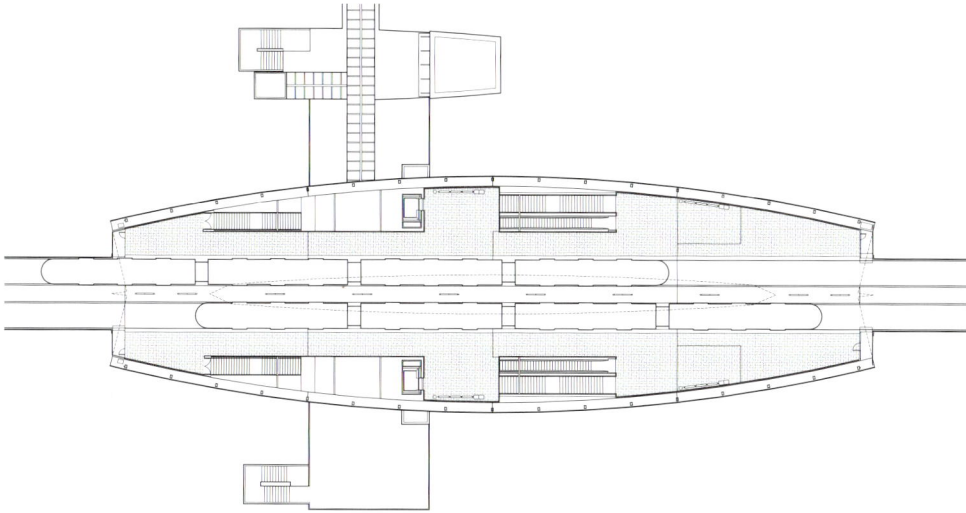

↓ | **View from ramp,** the mezzanine forms an open public space above the highway

Osterwold°Schmidt
EXP!ANDER Architekten BDA

↑ | **Passage**
→ | **Passage with planters**

Station square

Gotha

The rail station square terminal in Gotha makes direct changing between bus and train possible, providing a 50 by 50-meter PV panel roof and an illuminated stretched spread over the train platforms. A reference to Thuringian forest, the tourist destination BDA the street trolley, wooden terraces, clinker sitting areas and columned niches contrast with aluminum panels and profiled structural glass. The façade and roof are made of a PVDF-clad aluminum. The roof frame lies at a 6-meter elevation on supports of polished stainless steel. Protected open spaces with sitting arrangements on wood terraces offer an "urban living room" feel, enriching the quality of travelers' stay.

PROJECT FACTS

Address: Bahnhofstraße, 99867 Gotha, Germany. **Planning partner:** Torsten Braun (light designer), Hennicke+Dr.Kusch (structural engineer), IBP Erfurt (technical engineers). **Client:** Residenzstadt Gotha. **Completion:** 2008. **Type:** light rail. **Number of public levels:** 1. **Number of platforms:** 10. **Gross floor area:** 1,000 m². **Additional functions:** shops, offices. **Main materials:** exterior: stainless steel, aluminum PVDF, PVC luminous ceiling; interior: glass, mosaic, wood. **Setting:** inner city.

↑ | **View from station forecourt**
← | **Floor plan, platform level**

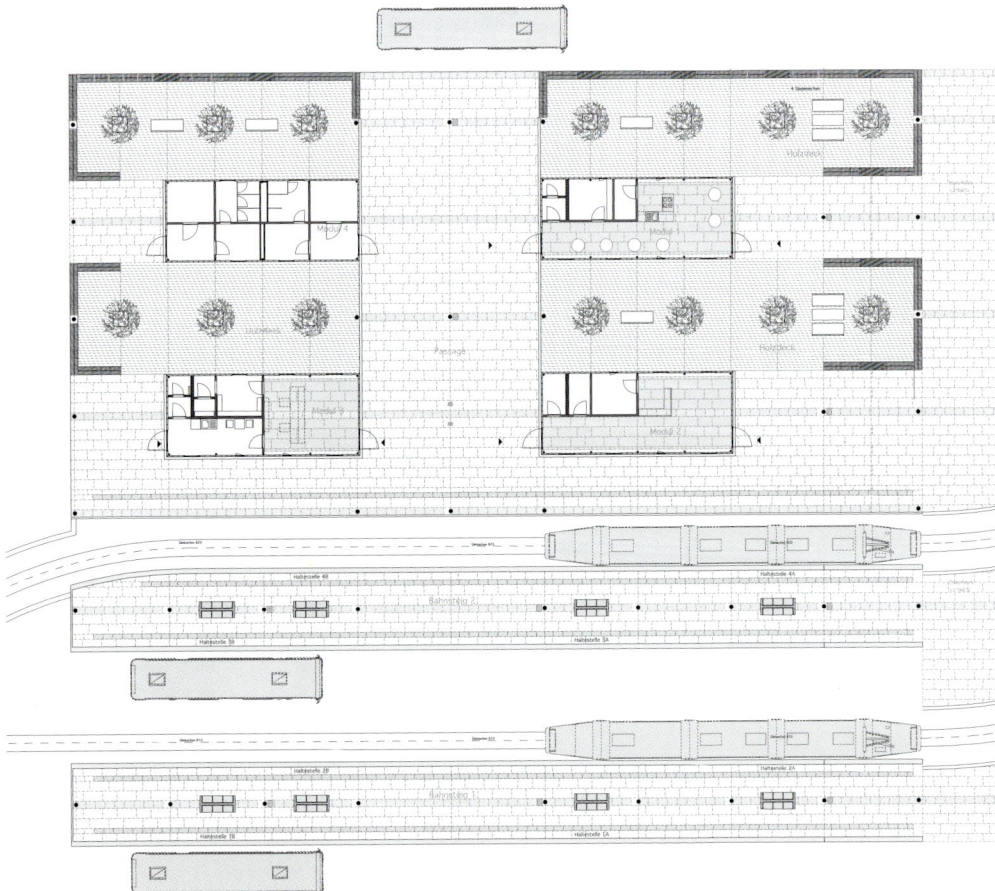

← | Detail façade
↓ | Passage with luminous ceiling

Arch. DI. Albert Wimmer

↑ | **Façade**, detail
↗ | **Night view from south**
→ | **Night view from east**

Praterstern station

Vienna

As a successor to the neglected Nordbahnhof of the 1960s, the new steel structure is one of Vienna's most modern traffic junctions. As a significant building in an elevated location it has become the identity-shaping signet for the city district. The building is distinguished by its easy accessibility, bright illumination and friendly atmosphere. This was achieved by the further development of two types of 19th century buildings, comfortable stations and noble arcades with contemporary architecture. At night, the façade is brightly illuminated like a crystal at the heart of the Praterstern area. The luxurious highly complex spatial complex resulted in a noble location which is the right of every human being, especially in the bustle of everyday life.

Address: Praterstern, 1020 Vienna, Austria. **Client:** ÖBB Infrastruktur BAU AG. **Completion:** 2008. **Type:** light rail. **Number of public levels:** 2. **Number of platforms:** 4. **Number of passengers per day:** 80,000. **Gross floor area:** 12,000 m². **Additional functions:** shops, restaurants. **Main materials:** exterior: double-glazing with expanded mesh aluminum spacers, fiberglass concrete slabs; interior: Tauerngrün natural stone (green serpentinite), fiberglass concrete slabs, anodized aluminum grid ceiling. **Setting:** urban.

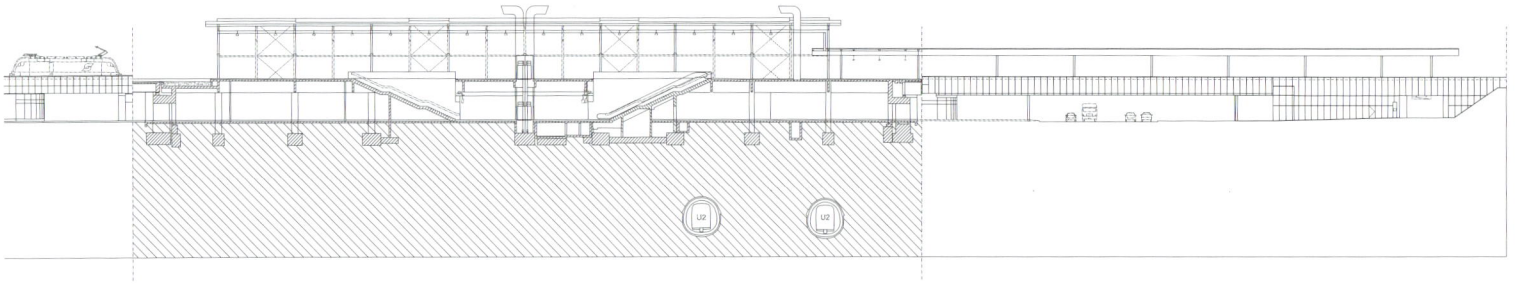

↑ | Longitudinal section
← | Tracks
↓ | Cross section

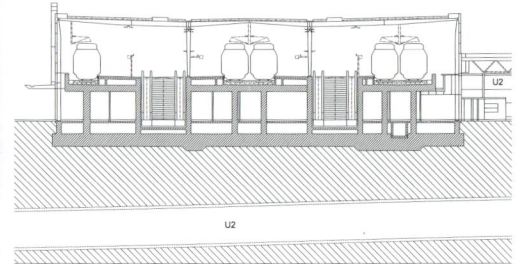

← | Station hall
↓ | Aerial view

↑ | **Passage ways,** on three levels
→ | **View along transitional axis**

Oriente station

Lisbon

The construction of a new rail and bus terminal on existing tracks, which cross the district along an embankment, was fundamental to the plan for a model district in an industrial wasteland in Lisbon. Calatrava placed the platforms on a bridge structure, comprised of five parallel rows of twinned arches. The bus terminal is located immediately to the west of the station, and a building complex is arranged around a plaza to the east. This plaza provides access to a shopping mall, which, along with ticket counters and platform access, occupies a multi-level hall directly beneath the platforms. Above the platforms, steel and glass "trees" interlock to form a continuous system of transparent roofs.

PROJECT FACTS

Address: Olivais District, 1800 Lisbon, Portugal. **Client:** Parque Expo '98. **Completion:** 1998. **Type:** light rail. **Number of public levels:** 3. **Number of platforms:** 5. **Additional functions:** bus station, shopping mall, park and ride facilities. **Main materials:** concrete, steel, glass. **Setting:** suburban.

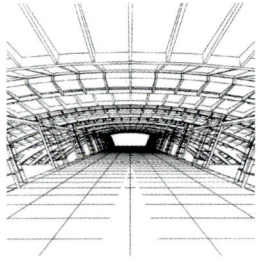

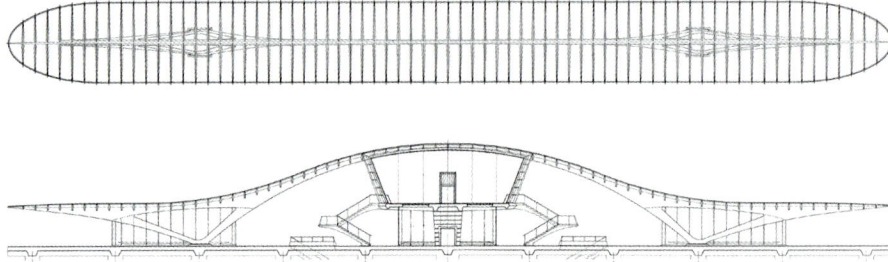

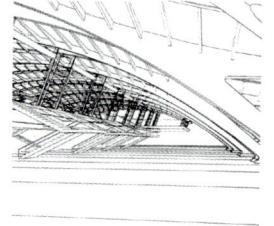

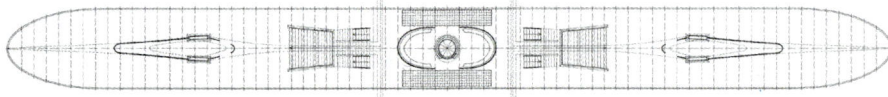

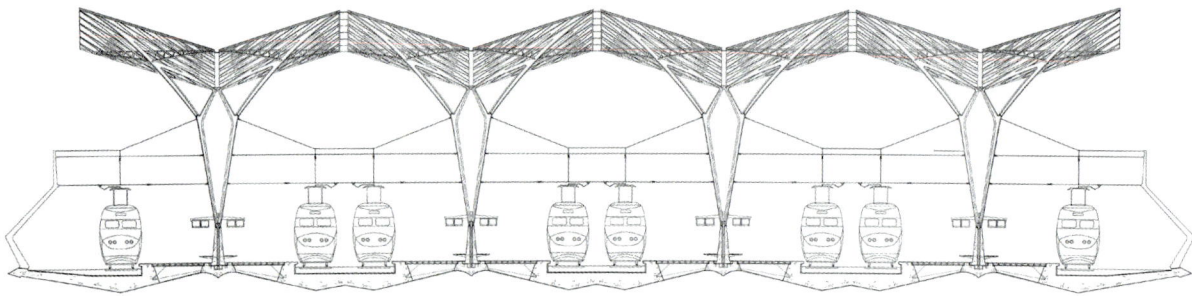

↑ | **Different elevations**
← | **Platforms,** roofed by glass and steel "trees"

← | **Perspective,** bus station in the foreground
↓ | **View at night,** entrance and illuminated roof

↑ | **Aerial view**
→ | **Light rail station,** view towards main building

Stratford DLR
London

The old Stratford DLR station, a four meter-wide single-track platform, was diagnosed as suffering from increasingly severe congestion at peak travel hours. Since the environs did not allow for broadening or enlargement of the existing station, a new station with an improved commuter capacity had to be constructed. The new DLR station is longer than its predecessor, allowing three train cars to dock. One of its most striking design features is the irregular structure of the outer skin, which consists of aluminum panel cladding. The platform provides a clear and inviting atmosphere as well as a high degree of passenger safety.

PROJECT FACTS
Address: Station St, Newham, London E15 1AZ, United Kingdom. **Client:** Transport for London.
Completion: 2007. **Type:** light rail. **Number of public levels:** 1. **Number of platforms:** 1. **Main materials:**
steel, concrete, aluminum, metal mesh. **Setting:** urban.

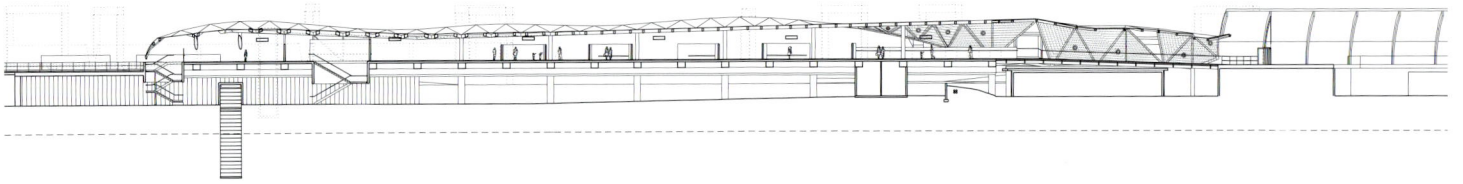
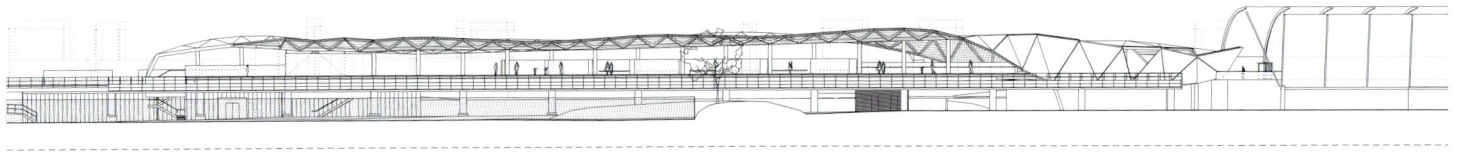

↑ | Longitudinal sections
← | Ceiling structure

← | **Detail,** signage
↓ | **Roof structure and cladding,** of the light rail station

Sasaki Associates

↑ | **View of service platform,** showing
structural ribs
→ | **View across platform**

CTC transit arena station

Charlotte

The station extends Sasaki's integrated team services for the Charlotte area's new Uptown
Corridor light rail system. Located adjacent to a new arena, a transportation terminal
and an entertainment center, the new transit station is the centerpiece of a major hub of
public activity bridging the boundaries of the uptown and downtown districts. The asym-
metrical design frames city skyline views to the north and provides an elevated viewing
platform for the cityscape to the south. Its roof cladding material integrates solar shad-
ing and transparency and allows for a lighter support structure. Color-shift LED lighting
transforms the station at night into a beacon and alerts passengers of train arrival.

PROJECT FACTS Address: 303 East Trade Street, Charlotte, NC 28202, USA. **Planning partner:** Arup (structural engineering), King Guinn Associates (structural engineering), Schweppe Lighting Design Inc. **Client:** Charlotte Area Transit System. **Completion:** 2007. **Type:** light rail. **Number of public levels:** 1. **Number of platforms:** 1. **Gross floor area:** 3,932 m². **Main materials:** glass, steel, brick. **Setting:** urban.

↑ | **Illuminated station** at night
← | **Station platform** at night

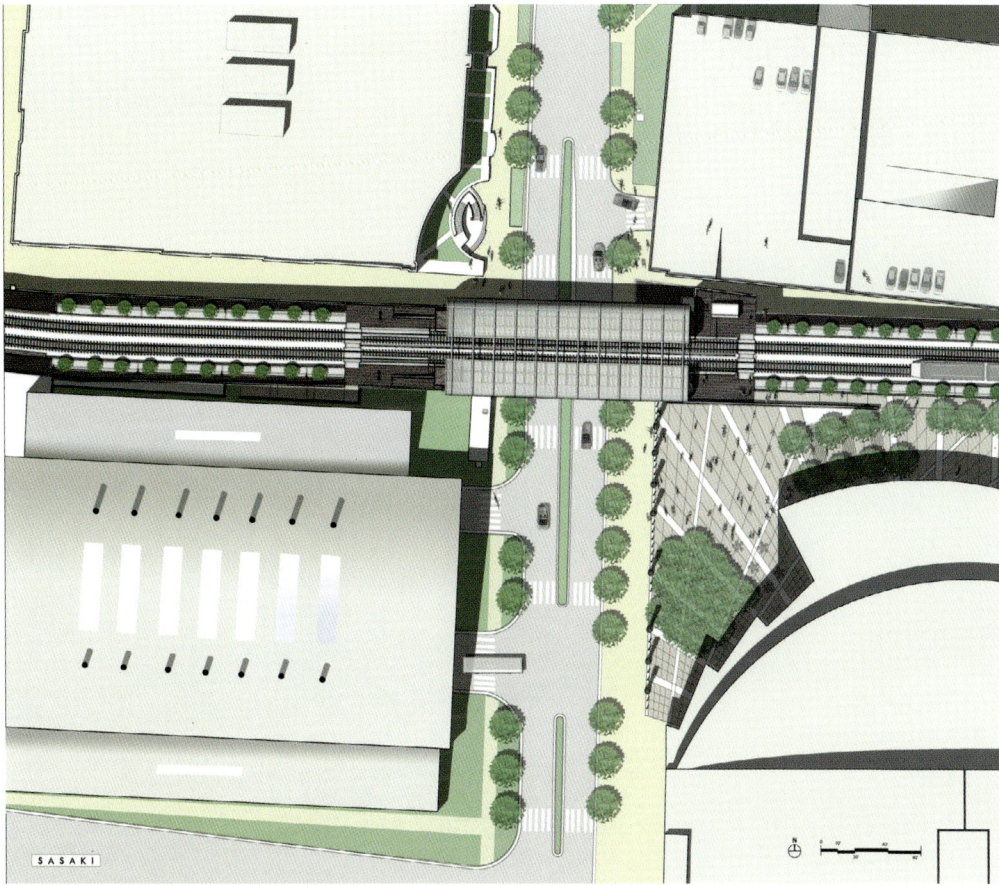

← | **Site plan**
↓ | **Station canopy** from East Trade Street

FXFOWLE Architects /
Sudhir Jambjekar

↑ | **Entrance area** at dusk
→ | **View along platform**

Bergenline Avenue tunnel station

Union City, NJ

For the new Hudson Bergen Light Rail Transit System, 12 stations were designed to link the urban towns of eastern New Jersey. Design guidelines were set to maintain a consistent look for the stations, but also to incorporate the local flavor of each station area. Sited atop the Palisades, New Jersey Transit's Bergenline Avenue tunnel station is a key intermodal node and the system's only tunnel station, with the platform located 160 feet below grade. At the plaza level, access to the platform below is provided by elevators within a brick and glass head house structure, flanked by ventilation stacks and a sleek glass canopy. Site specific art installations were integrated into the design.

PROJECT FACTS

Address: Bergenline Avenue, Union City, NJ 07087, USA. **Client:** New Jersey Transit. **Completion:** 2005. **Type:** light rail. **Number of public levels:** 2. **Number of platforms:** 2. **Additional functions:** staff facilities, bus station. **Main materials:** concrete, brick, aluminum, glass. **Setting:** inner city.

← | **Façade at night,** brickwork and aluminum

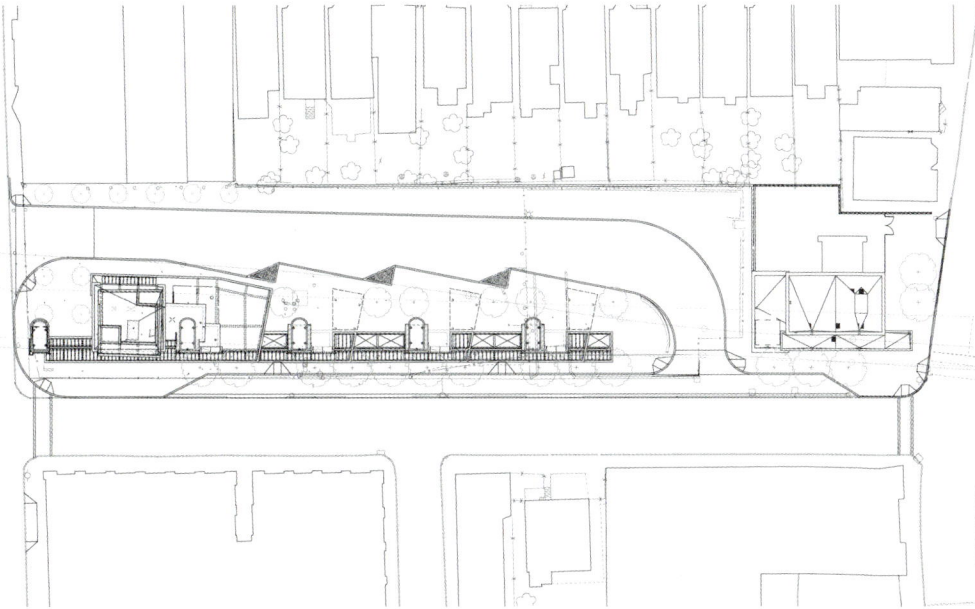

← | Site plan
↓ | View along platform

↑ | **Station Oosterheem,** regional trains on ground level and metro above
→ | **On the platform,** station Willem Dreeslaan

Oosterheem line

Zoetermeer

The Oosterheemlijn is part of a new network of light rail connections between Rotterdam, The Hague and Zoetermeer, an expanding neighborhood in the polders that has grown into a regular town. The Oosterheemlijn crosses several different (urban) landscapes such as drained polders and areas that have always been dry. The line is meant to move quietly and discreetly through both city and countryside and therefore a clear, well-defined and slender design has been developed, making the line a recognizable and autonomous part of the surroundings. A single, clearly distinguished design was applied to the constructional works, underpasses and stations, applying uniform materials and techniques.

PROJECT FACTS
Address: Zoetermeer, The Netherlands. **Client:** City of Zoetermeer. **Completion:** 2008. **Type:** light rail.
Number of public levels: 1. **Number of platforms:** 2. **Main materials:** stainless steel, concrete, glass,
tiles. **Setting:** suburban.

↑ | **Station from below**
← | **Stairs,** to the platforms

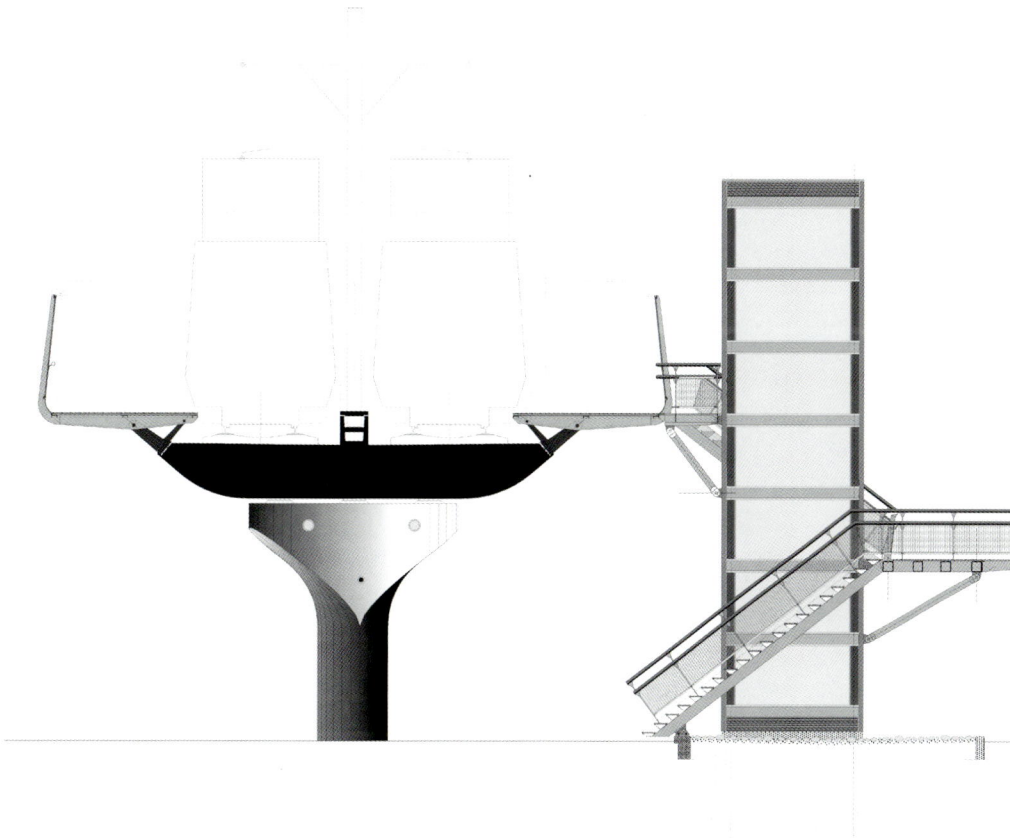

← | Section
↓ | One of the train bridges

Underground Light Rail

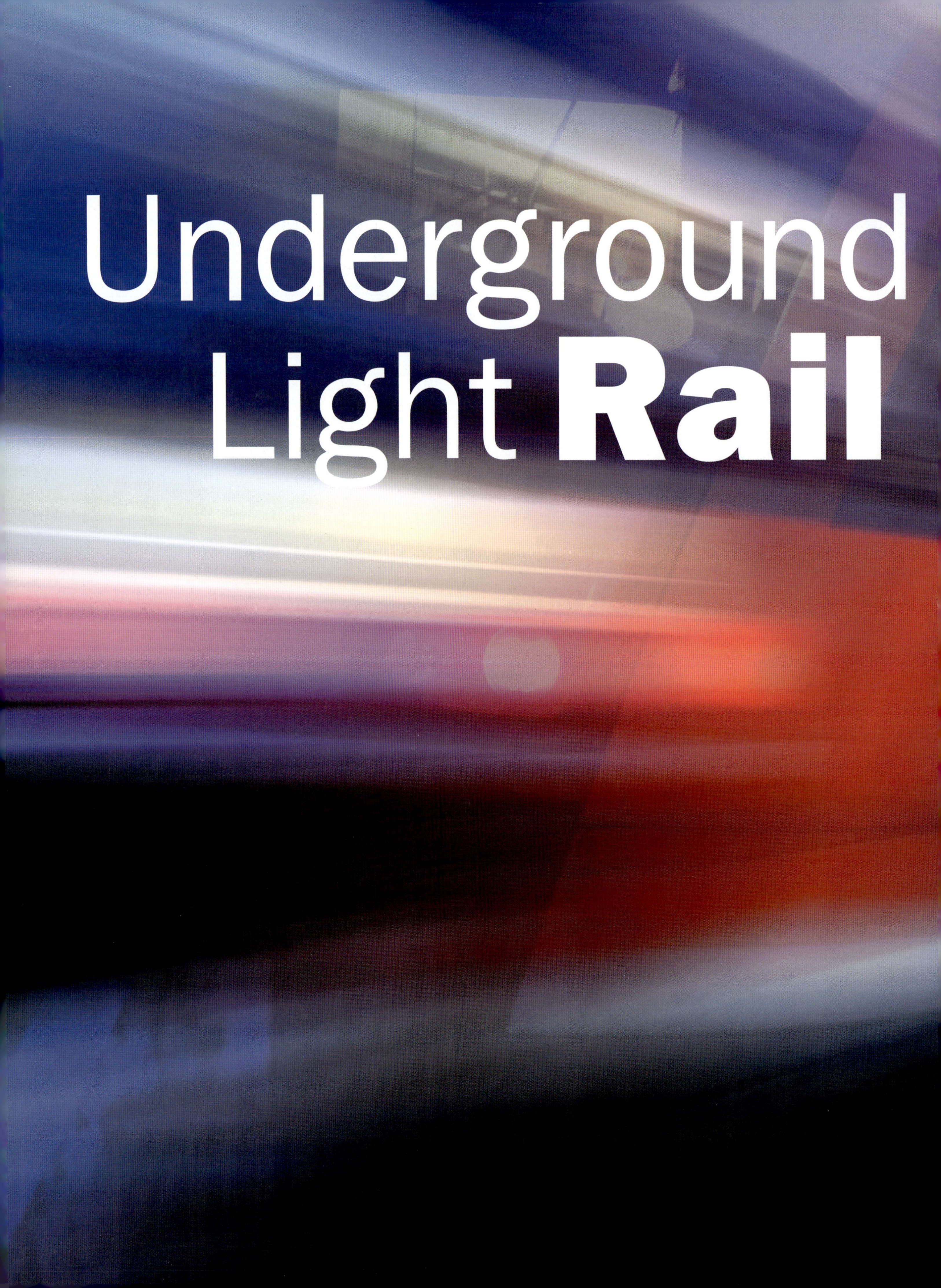

↑ | **View over platforms**

Bilbao metro

Bilbao

In contrast to other transit systems, the Bilbao metro was conceived as a totality from the start – a shared vision of architectural, engineering and construction skills. The construction of tunnels leading underground was given the same importance as the development of the public areas. The design attempts to achieve a degree of architectural legibility which offers travelers orientation beyond the scope of the signage system. Typical for the Bilbao metro are cavernous stations, big enough to accommodate lightweight stainless steel mezzanines and staircases above the trains. A further striking feature are curved glass structures which announce the inner-city stations along Line 1.

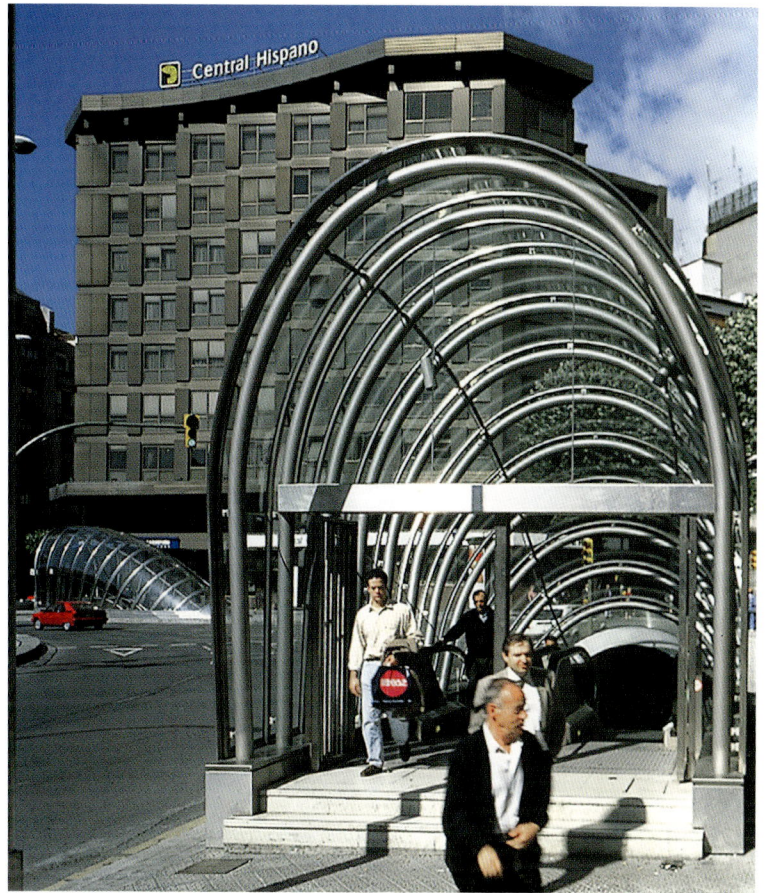

PROJECT FACTS

Address: Lehendakari Agirre, 48015 Bilbao, Spain. Client: Bilbao metro. Completion: 2010. Type: light rail. Number of public levels: 2. Number of platforms: 2. Main materials: steel, glass, concrete, stone. Setting: inner city.

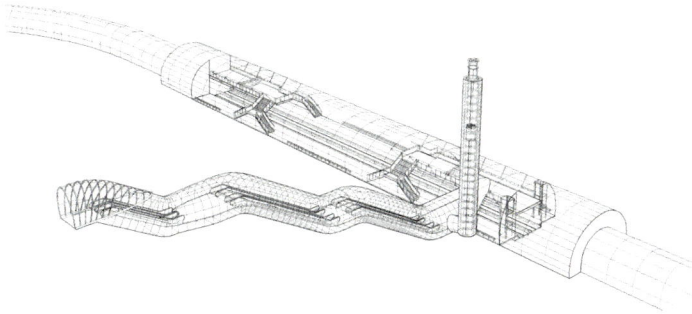

↑ | Plan
↓ | View upstairs

↑ | Entrance

↑ | **Bird's-eye view** of station entrances in front of the city hall,
with tramline as a future option

Station Rotes Rathaus
Berlin

"Berliner Rathaus" is the first station of the extended U5 subway line from Alexanderplatz to Berlin central station. In terms of urban design it constitutes a respectful reference to the prominent town hall façade. Entrances are reduced to a minimum and not roofed, so as not to compete with the town hall architecture. The open layout and consistent use of materials create palpable relationships between the train platform and the exterior space, resulting in a spatial unit with a clear structure. The open design of the entrances provides daylight underground and good visual connections, while passengers can easily find their way around with a strong subjective sense of security.

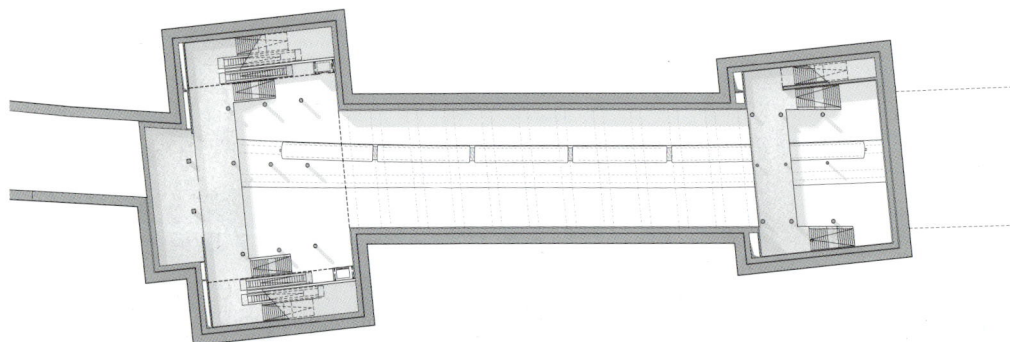

PROJECT FACTS

Address: Rathausstraße 15, 10178 Berlin, Germany. **Planning partner:** Zerna Ingenieure GmbH / CDM (construction); BVG (consultant), Bünck+Fehse (visualization). **Client:** Berliner Verkehrsbetriebe (BVG). **Completion:** 2017. **Type:** light rail. **Number of public levels:** 2. **Number of platforms:** 2. **Number of passengers per day:** 120,000. **Gross floor area:** 10,000 m². **Additional functions:** shop. **Main materials:** concrete stone, terrazzo, glass. **Setting:** inner city.

↑ | **Platform, stairs and elevator**
↙ | **Floor plan,** underground level

↓ | **View from landing**

Rogers, Stirk, Harbour +
Partners / Richard Rogers

↑ | **Huge canopy** resting on yellow trees
→ | **View from below**

R9 station

Kaohsiung

This station will serve Kaohsiung's popular Central Park and the adjacent shopping district. The design of R9 seeks to pull the park's landscaping into the station through the main entrance. A sloped, green bank guides passengers down to the concourse level, some eleven meters below ground level. Two sets of escalators, plus linear staircases to either side, allow people to move between the concourse level and the park. A large aluminum canopy spans the entire below-ground concourse, protecting this area from strong sunlight and rainfall. The roof is designed as a curved, stressed-skin monocoque. The trapezoid canopy is perforated with glazed openings to allow daylight penetration.

PROJECT FACTS
Address: Kaohsiung, Taiwan. **Planning partner:** Resource Engineering Service, Inc., Structured Environment. **Client:** Kaohsiung Rapid Transit Corporation. **Completion:** 2007. **Type:** light rail. **Number of public levels:** 3. **Number of platforms:** 2. **Gross floor area:** 14,300 m². **Main materials:** aluminum, steel, concrete. **Setting:** suburban.

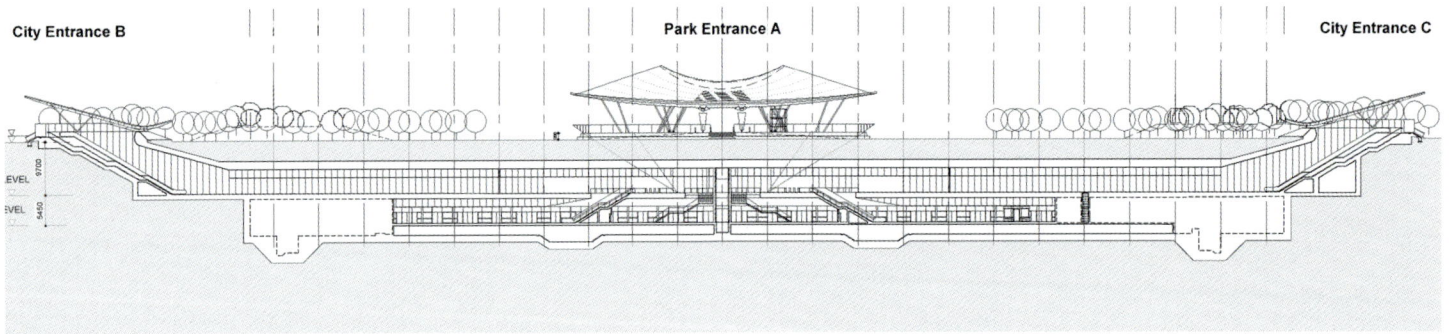

City Entrance B

Park Entrance A

City Entrance C

↑ | **Section**
← | **Distant view** from opposite street side

← | **Canopy at dusk,** view from below
↓ | **Perspective at night**

Kuryłowicz &
Associates Architecture

↑ | **Entrance area,** at dusk

Dworzec Gdañski metro

Warsaw

This metro station is located in the northern part of Warsaw, adjacent to the Gdañska railway station. It is not only one of the city's major transportation hubs, but also serves as a pedestrian underpass below Słomiñskiego Street. Both ends of the 120-meter long station are equipped with stairs, escalators as well as elevators. Smooth surfaces of polished stone or aluminum and a well-balanced illumination result in a friendly and clean atmosphere. The station is clearly structured to allow passengers and commuters to easily orient themselves and to achieve a high degree of safety. The gallery above the station features shops, a ticket counter and a police station.

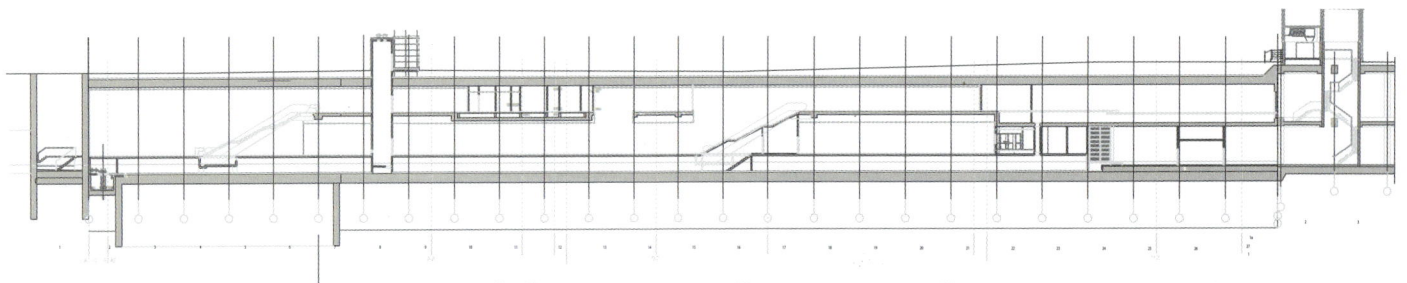

Address: Zygmunta Słomińskiego 4, 00-204 Warsaw, Poland. **Client:** Metro Warszawskie. **Completion:** 2003. **Type:** light rail. **Number of public levels:** 2. **Number of platforms:** 1. **Additional functions:** shops, police station. **Main materials:** stone, steel, aluminum, glass. **Setting:** urban.

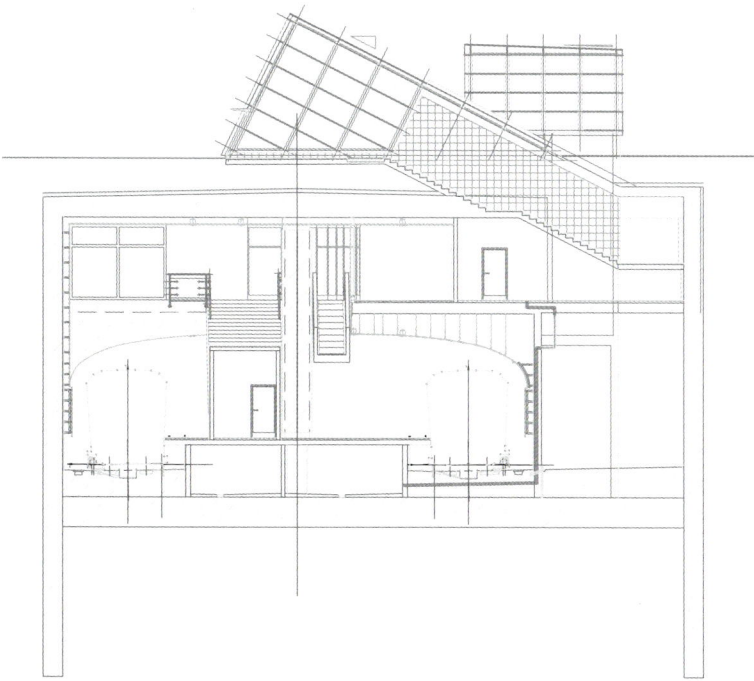

↑ | Cross section
↙ | Longitudinal section

↑ | View along platform
↓ | View into the underpass

↑ | **Ticket hall,** Blackfriars Road

Southwark station, Jubilee line extension

London

The main objective of the design for the new Southwark station was to maximize passenger comfort and security by minimizing the complexity of the station. This was achieved by distinguishing and enhancing the volumetric characteristics of passenger areas. The station comprises several distinctly different spaces. The principle behind these varied and spatially diverse areas is to respect and respond to the civil engineering envelope developed with the engineers. The progress of passengers from the ground level to the platform in an easy and clear fashion is paramount, while the generosity of the public spaces is enhanced by the applied materials and finishes.

PROJECT FACTS
Address: Blackfriars Road, London, SE1 8NW, United Kingdom. **Client:** London Underground Limited. **Completion:** 1999. **Type:** light rail. **Number of public levels:** 2. **Number of platforms:** 2. **Main materials:** aluminum, steel, concrete, glass. **Setting:** urban.

↑ | Escalator
↓ | Section

↑ | Lower concourse

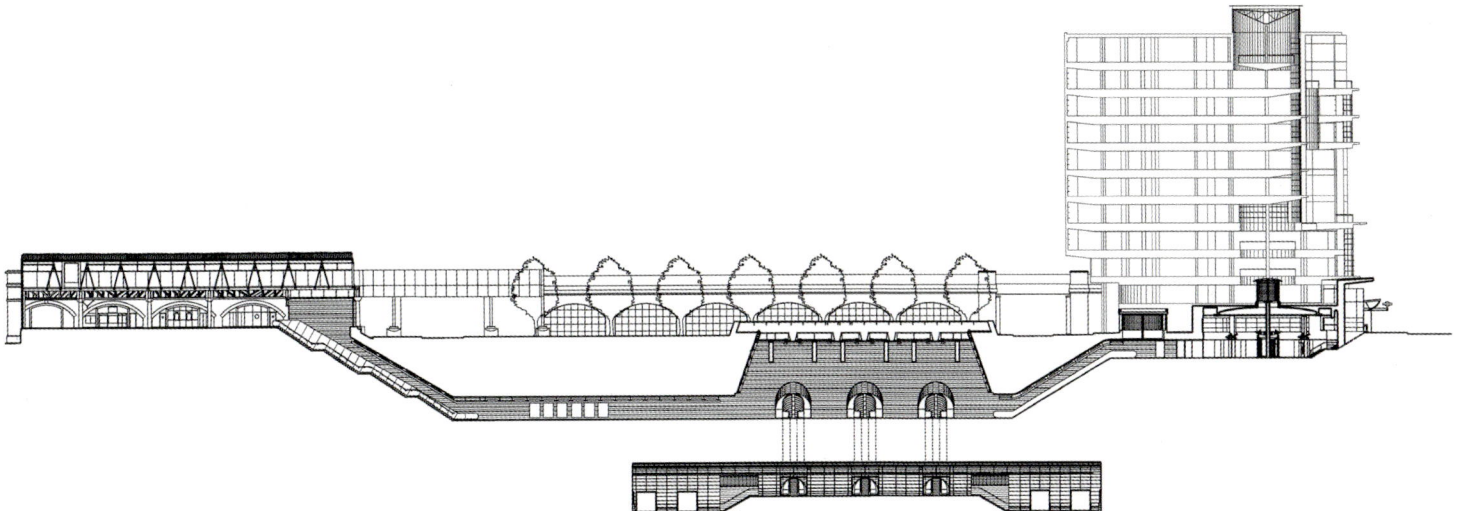

Architektengruppe U-Bahn (AGU) / Wilhelm Holzbauer, Heinz Marschalek, Georg Ladstätter, Bert Gantar

↑ | **Station Kagraner Platz**, U1 Nord

Metro lines U1, U3, U4 and U6
Vienna

The architects developed a universal panel system, which was used to create flexible passages, corridors, stairwells as well as platforms. Ticket machines, seats, waste bins, ash trays, doors, as well as information, orientation and safety elements are all part of the system as well and may be easily exchanged thanks to their uniform sizes. The design strictly separates between the darker and unpolished rail area and the lighter and more colorful communication areas, where the curved end of the ceiling above the platform edge, together with a strip of light, signify the edge of the danger zone. Individual colors serve not only as a guiding system, but also determine each line's image.

PROJECT FACTS

Address: Vienna, Austria. **Client:** City of Vienna, Wiener Linien. **Completion:** 2015. **Type:** light rail. **Number of passengers per day:** 2,000,000. **Additional functions:** shops. **Main materials:** exterior: glass, aluminum, enameled steel panels; interior: enameled steel panels, aluminum. **Setting:** inner city, urban, suburban.

↑ | **Station Rennbahnweg,** U1 Nord
↓ | **Station Kagraner Platz,** U1 Nord

↑ | **Station Rennbahnweg,** U1 Nord
↓ | **Station Leopoldau,** U1 Nord

↑ | **Station Hietzing, U4**
↓ | **Cross section**

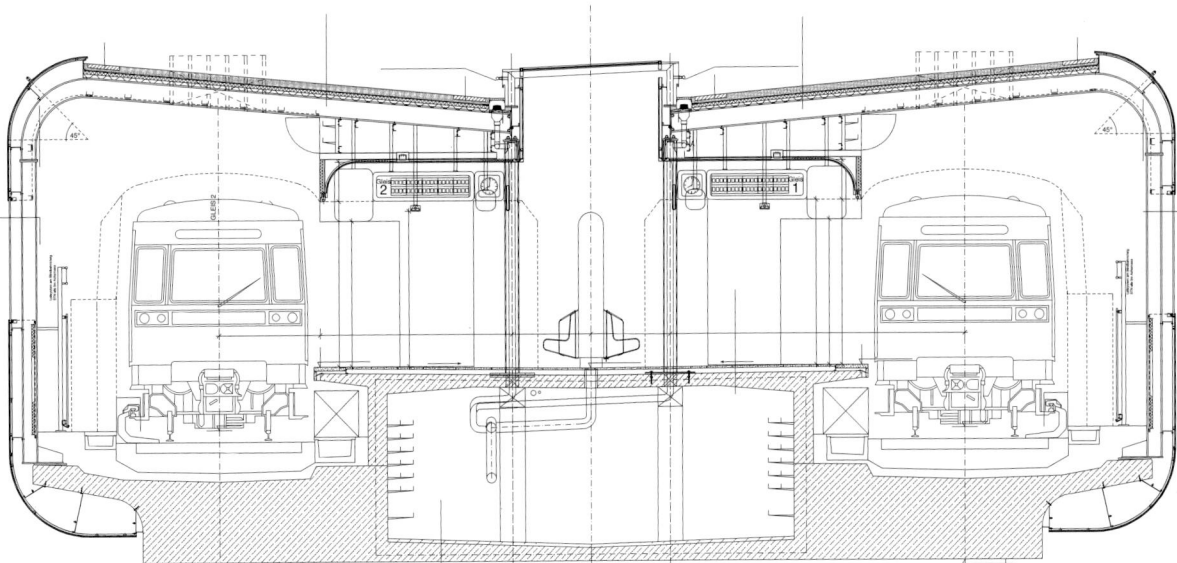

← | **Station Gasometer**, U3
↓ | **Station Stockholmer Platz**, U1

↑ | **Way down to the platform**
→ | **Platform,** decorated with printed ceramic

Metro 4 stations
Gellért tér and Fővám tér
Budapest

The ten stations on either side of the Danube River have been constructed as the first stage of a project creating a new metro line connecting South-Buda with the city center. Proximity to the Danube and other plot requirements necessitated complex structural solutions for Szent Gellért tér and Fővám tér stations. The stations consist of a cut-and-cover box and tunnels. An additional tunnel for the tramline and a new pedestrian subway has to be constructed for the Fővám tér station. With the new underground station, Fővám tér will become a new gateway to the historic downtown Pest.

PROJECT FACTS

Address: Szent Gellért tér, Fővám tér, 1093 Budapest, Hungary. **General design:** Palatium Stúdió Kft. **Aplied art:** Tamás Komoróczky. **Client:** Budapest Transport Ltd., DBR Metro Project Directory. **Completion:** 2012. **Type:** light rail. **Number of public levels:** 3. **Number of platforms:** 1. **Number of passengers per day:** 30,000. **Gross floor area:** 7,100 m². **Main materials:** exterior: concrete, glass; interior: concrete, corten steel, printed ceram. **Setting:** inner city, urban.

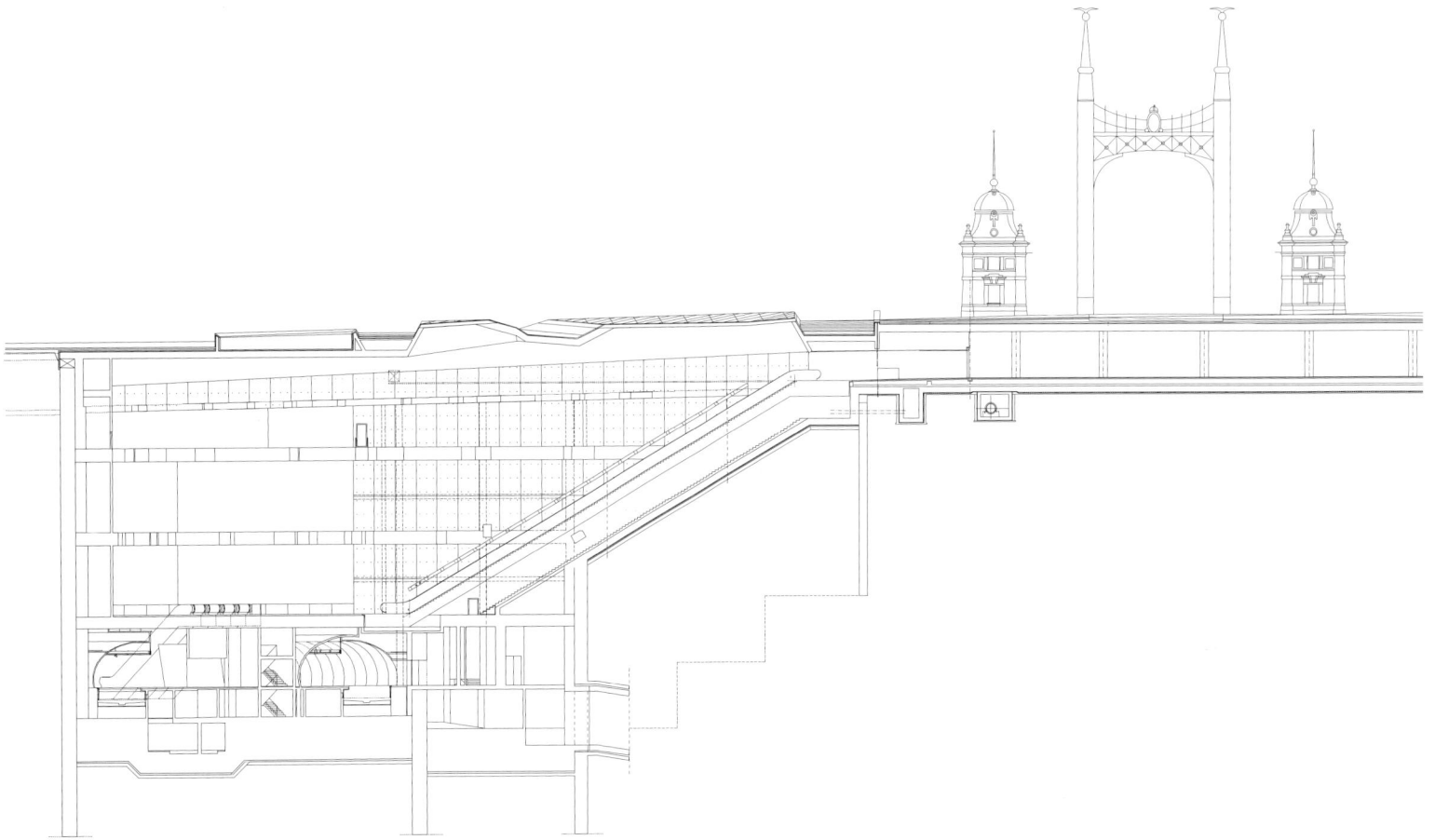

↑ | Section
← | Aesthetic statics

← | Inner space
↓ | Floor plan platform level

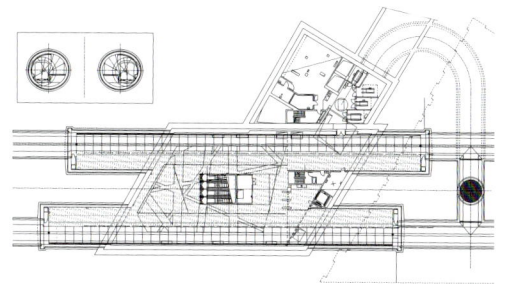

↑ | View along platform
→ | View towards escalators

Underground line U2
Schottenring to Messe

Vienna

The principle of bringing natural light to the platform level is an important characteristic and identifying feature of the new U2 underground stations. This design concept strengthens spatial perception and aids orientation below ground. Near-surface stations allow visual communication with the street level through light wells above platforms. In low-lying stations, the descent to the underground platforms is orchestrated using sculptural stairwells and gorge-like escalator shafts. These spaces are formed using exposed concrete, while accessible areas utilize enamel cladding, steel accents and granite floors.

PROJECT FACTS **Address:** Districts 1010 and 1020 Vienna, Austria. **Planning partner:** Architect Paul Katzberger. **Client:** Wiener Linien GmbH & Co KG. **Completion:** 2008. **Type:** light rail. **Number of passengers per day:** 90,000. **Main materials:** concrete, enamel, steel, granite. **Setting:** inner city.

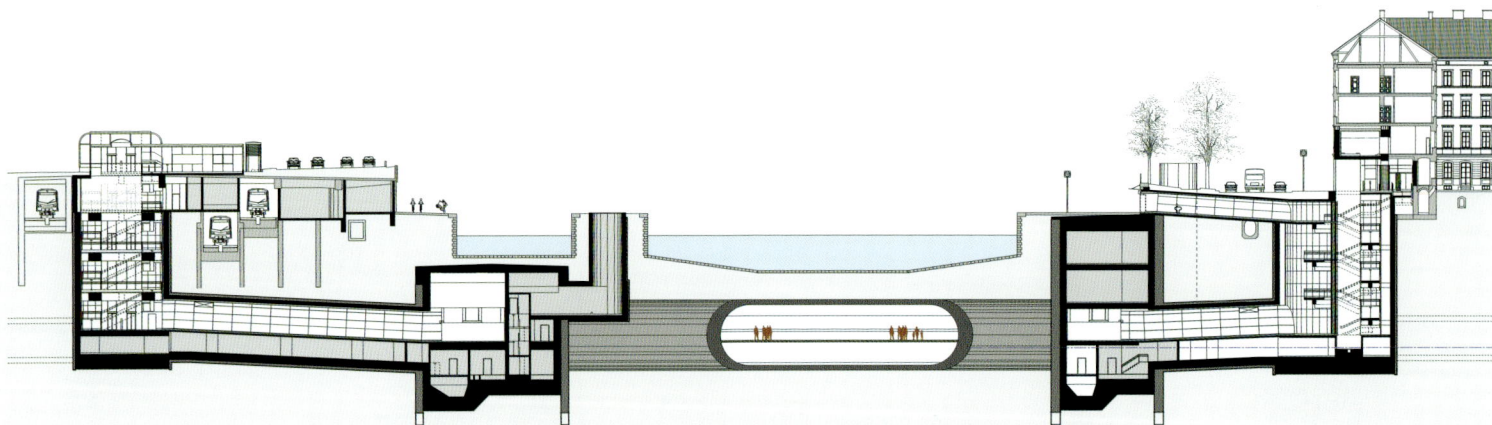

↑ | Section
← | Stairs

← | View towards rooflight

↑ | **Platforms** of the light rail station
→ | **Interior view,** friendly atmosphere through decoration and illumination

Modal transit station

San Diego

The underground tunnel station and bus transit center for the San Diego Trolley is part of the new 5.5-mile Mission Valley East light rail alignment. The new line connects San Diego State University to Qualcomm Stadium znd downtown. It places regional light rail service at the very heart of San Diego State University, while simultaneously enhancing open space, pedestrian connections and campus redevelopment. The station provides a convenient transit alternative for students who previously commuted to campus by car. By acknowledging the sloping grade of the adjacent campus green space, one side of the station platform is transformed from "below grade" to "at grade," allowing daylight to penetrate inside.

Address: 5500 Campanile Drive, San Diego, CA 92182, USA. **Planning partner:** Anne Mudge, Estrada Land Planning, Lloyd D. Lindley, ASLA. **Client:** TriMet. **Completion:** 2009. **Type:** light rail. **Number of public levels:** 3. **Additional functions:** park. **Main materials:** steel, stone. **Setting:** urban.

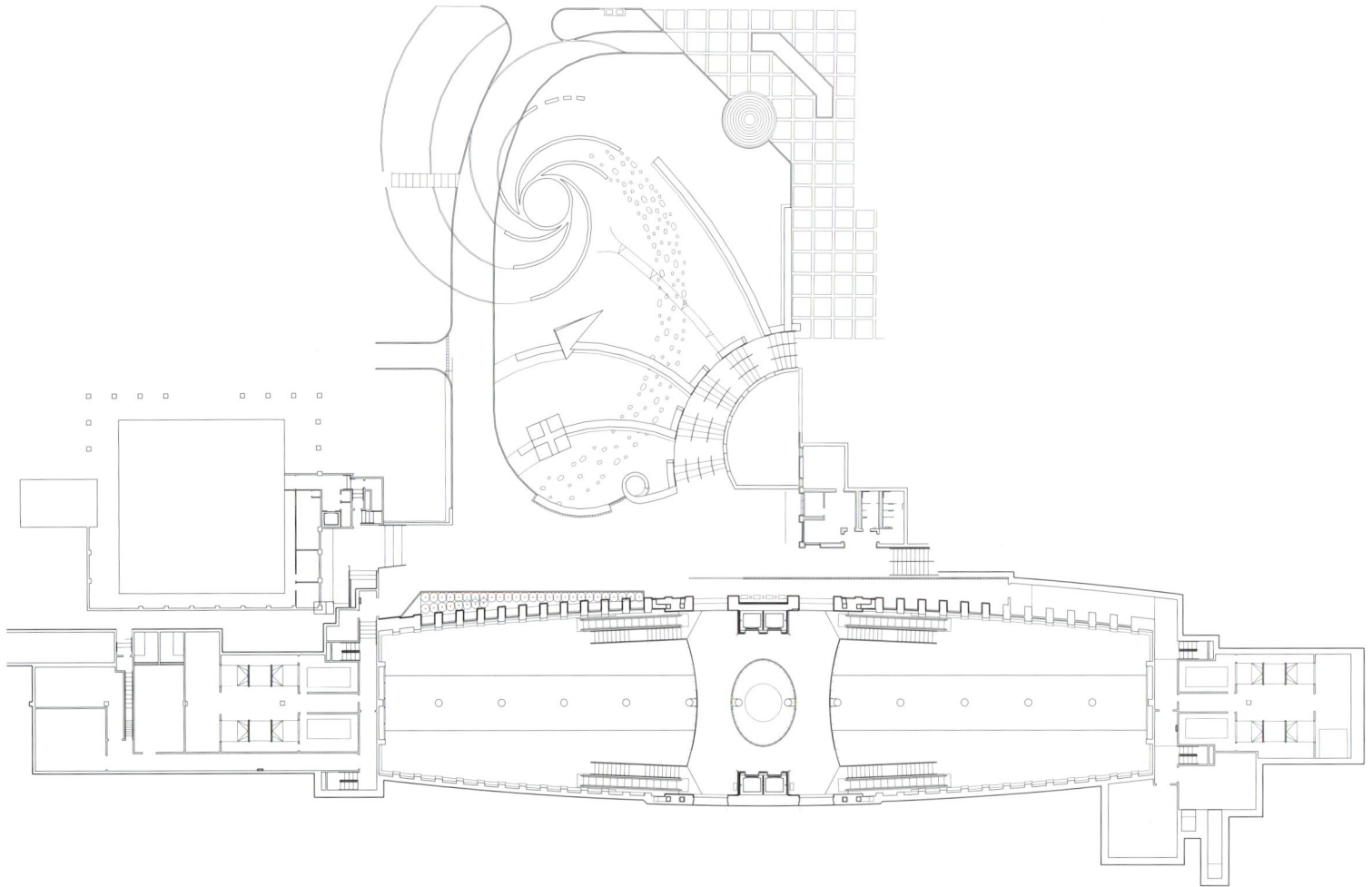

↑ | **Site plan**
← | **Pedestrian routes** at different levels

← | View along the façade
↓ | Bird's-eye view

Hawkins Brown Architects /
Roger Hawkins, Russell
Brown, David Bickle

↑ | TCR Crossrail Eastern ticket hall

Tottenham Courtroad station upgrade

London

One of the busiest underground stations serving approximately 100,000 passengers a day in Central London needed a new ticket hall, six times the size of the original facilities. New lifts were incorporated to enable barrier-free access from the public realm to the platforms. Once finished, this station will operate as the TCR Crossrail Eastern ticket hall. Hawkins/Brown were additionally engaged by Transport for London to prepare proposals for a new pedestrian plaza which incorporates two new entrances. Art on the Underground commissioned Daniel Buren to collaborate with the architects on a series of station installations to aid passenger orientation.

Address: Tottenham Court Road, Westminster, London W1, United Kingdom. **Planning partner:** Halcrow. **Artist:** Daniel Buren. **Client:** London Underground. **Completion:** 2016. **Type:** light rail. **Number of passengers per day:** 200,000. **Main materials:** steel, concrete, glass. **Setting:** urban.

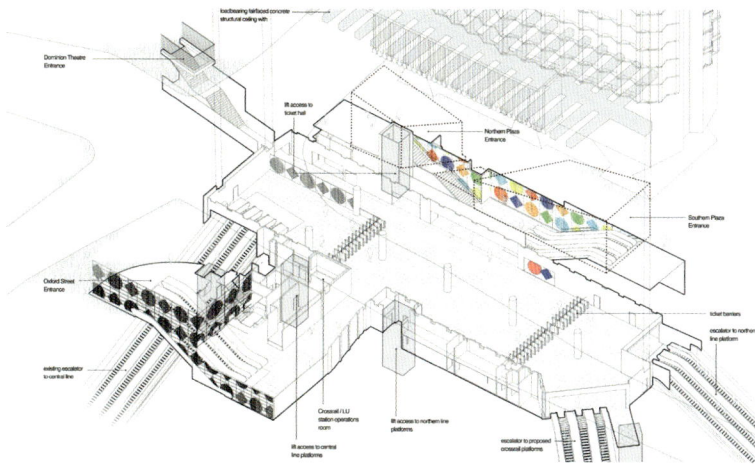

↑ | Plan
↓ | Front façade

↑ | Entrance

Santiago Calatrava
Architect & Engineer

↑ | **Perspective view** of the structure
→ | **Side elevation,** showing the structural ridges reaching towards the sky

WTC transportation hub
New York, NY

The project's ambition is to trigger the redevelopment of this New York quarter, destroyed in the September 11 attacks. Functionally, the hub's primary purpose is to significantly improve transit connections across Lower Manhattan while serving as a global unifying element, linking buildings and squares on the site. The transit hub is perceived as a series of three spaces that are necessarily different from each other, one being a linear vault, another a trapezoidal large-span hall and the last a high-arched atrium. Unifying treatments of structural typology, color and materials employed by the buildings define them as a sequence of events for the user. Two themes for creating well-lit open spaces with a minimized number of internal supports run throughout the project.

PROJECT FACTS

Address: Ground Zero, New York, NY 10001-1303, USA. **Planning partner:** Downtown Design Partnership. **Client:** Port Authority of New York and New Jersey. **Completion:** 2015. **Type:** light rail (subway and PATH trains). **Additional functions:** shopping mall, public square. **Main materials:** concrete, steel, stone, glass. **Setting:** inner city.

↑ | **Interior view,** well lit ambience
← | **Interior view** of Path hall

← | Sketch
↓ | Perspective view

ON-A / Eduardo Gutierrez,
Jordi Fernandez

↑ | **Access** to tunnel interconnection
→ | **Access from Ramblas,** white concrete in
contrast with dark ceiling

Metro station Drassanes

Barcelona

The designers in charge of refurbishing the Drassanes metro station were faced with the double constraints of limited available space and pre-existing station components. For this reason, the new skin of the station had to accommodate restricted space and include all previous installations while giving way to new functions. As a guiding visual concept, the designers chose the interior of an existing train car with the assumption that it already contains all the elements necessary for passengers. The white, glass-reinforced concrete used as the surface material is both resistant to abrasions from daily use and provides a light and clean atmosphere.

PROJECT FACTS

Address: Drassanes, 08001, Barcelona, Spain. **Client:** Transports Metropolitans de Barcelona. **Completion:** 2009. **Type:** light rail. **Number of public levels:** 2. **Number of platforms:** 2. **Gross floor area:** 1,500 m². **Main materials:** glass reinforced concrete. **Setting:** inner city.

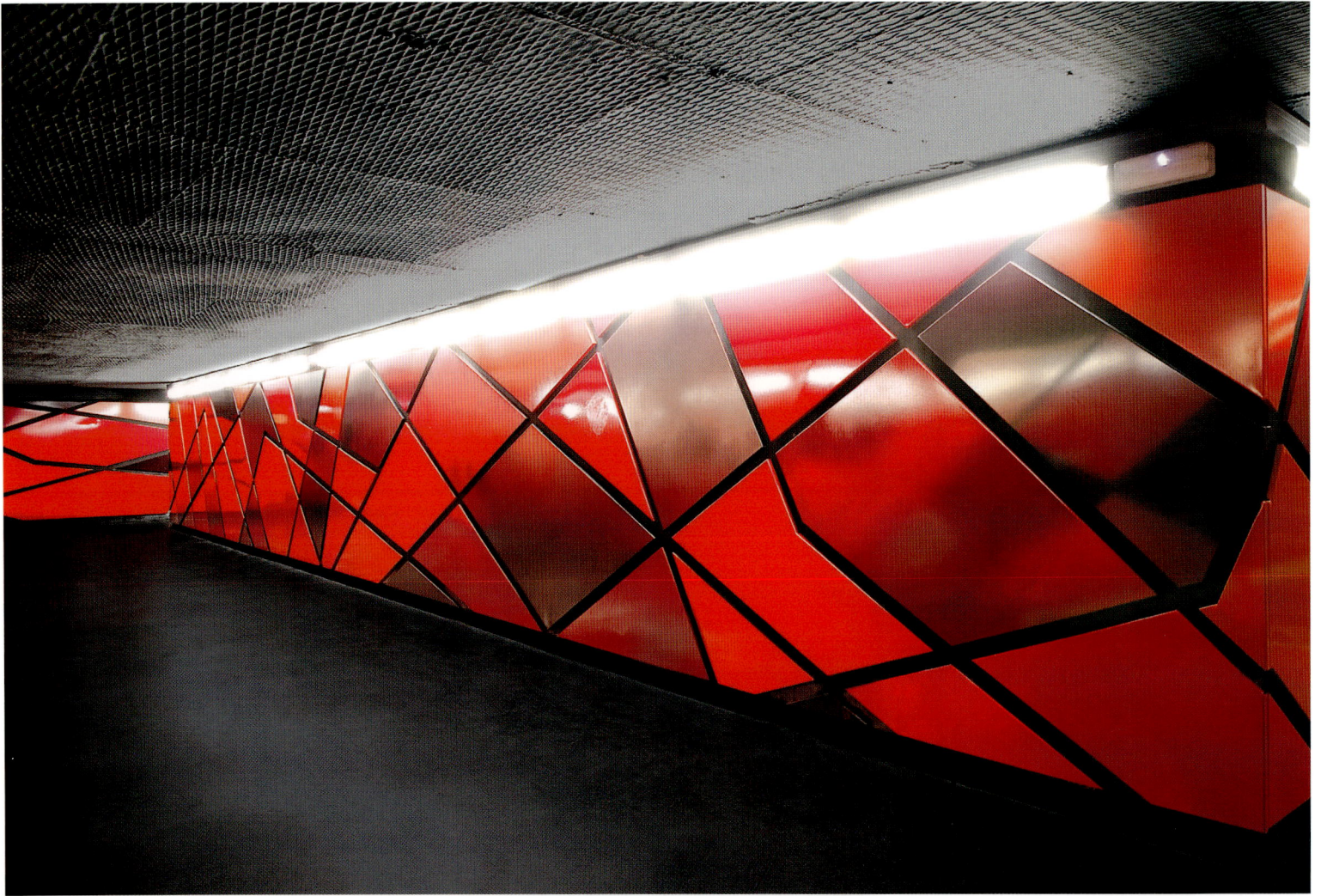

↑ | **Colorful mosaic** within interconnection tunnel
← | **Detail** of mosaic wall

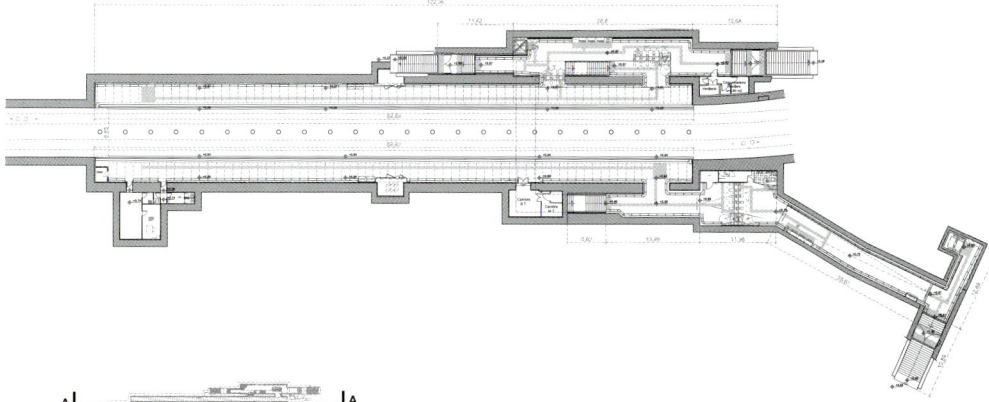

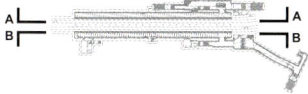

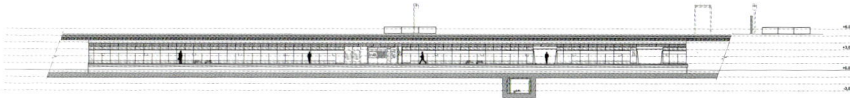

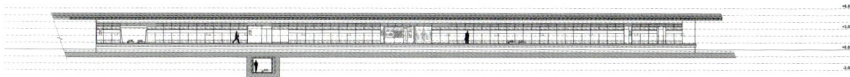

← | Plan and sections
↓ | View along the platform

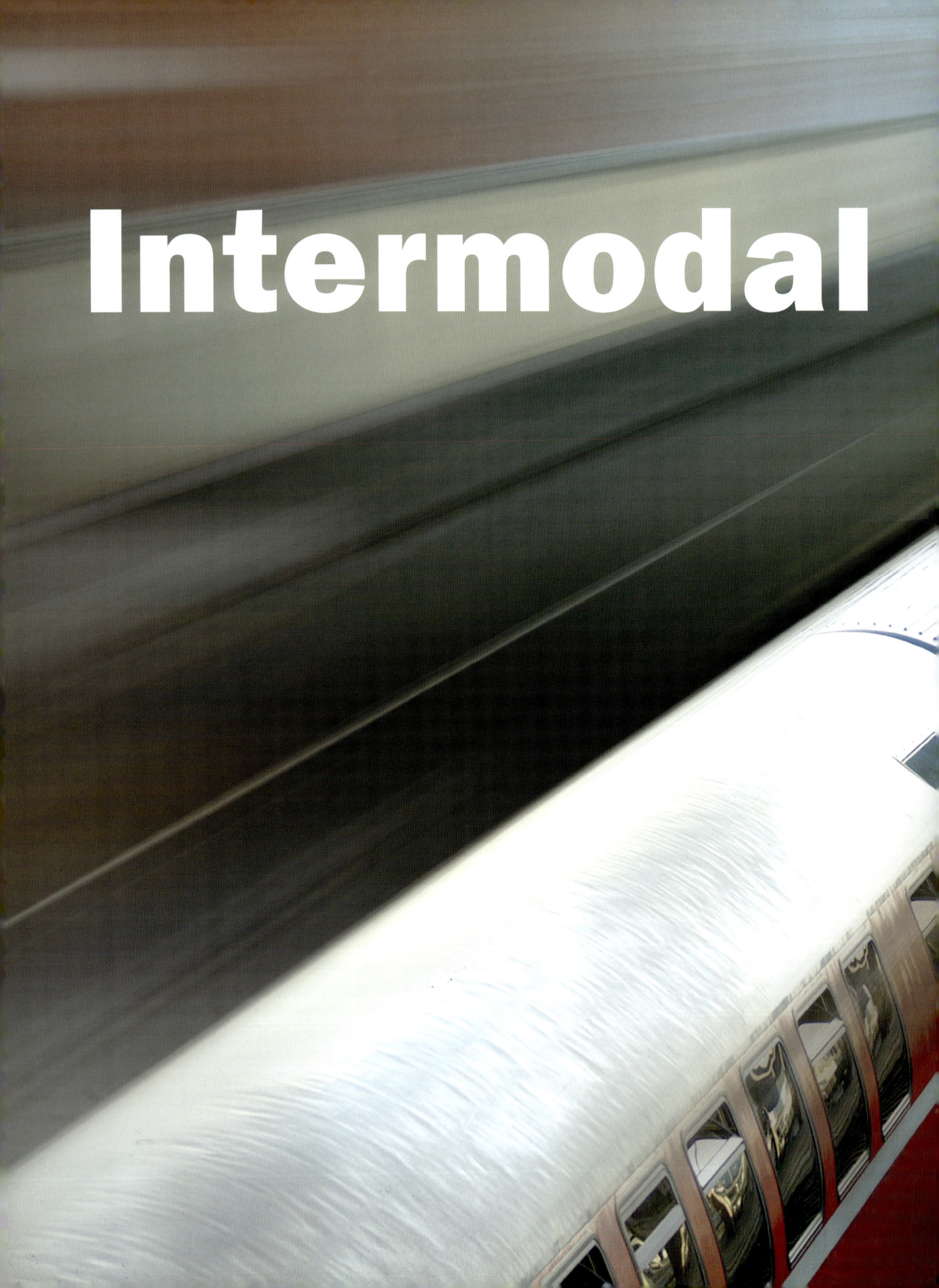

Intermodal

gmp – von Gerkan,
Marg and Partners
Architects

↑ | **Perspective view**
↓ | **Section**

→ | **Different levels** of the station

Berlin main station

Berlin

Europe's largest train station for long-distance, regional and local transit is located in Berlin's Tiergarten area. This is where the belowground north-south high-speed train track and the arching route of the east-west rails intersect. Bidirectional commuter rail lines and a metro line traveling in the north-south direction connect here as well. The design's main principle is the immediately apparent emphasis on the course of the tracks within the urban space. Large scale filigree glass roofs and two bridging office towers communicate this idea using architectural means. The two office buildings slice into the east-west track structure like bridges.

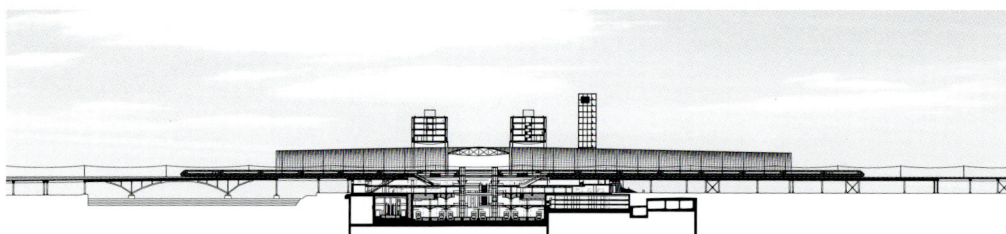

PROJECT FACTS

Address: Invalidenstraße 53, 10557 Berlin-Tiergarten, Germany. **Client:** Deutsche Bahn AG. **Completion:** 2006. **Type:** light and heavy rail. **Number of public levels:** 5. **Number of platforms:** 7. **Number of passengers per day:** 25,000. **Gross floor area:** 175,000 m². **Additional functions:** shopping mall, offices. **Main materials:** glass, steel, concrete, natural stone, wood. **Setting:** inner city.

↑ | **Glass façade** at the main entrance
← | **Detail** of glass façade

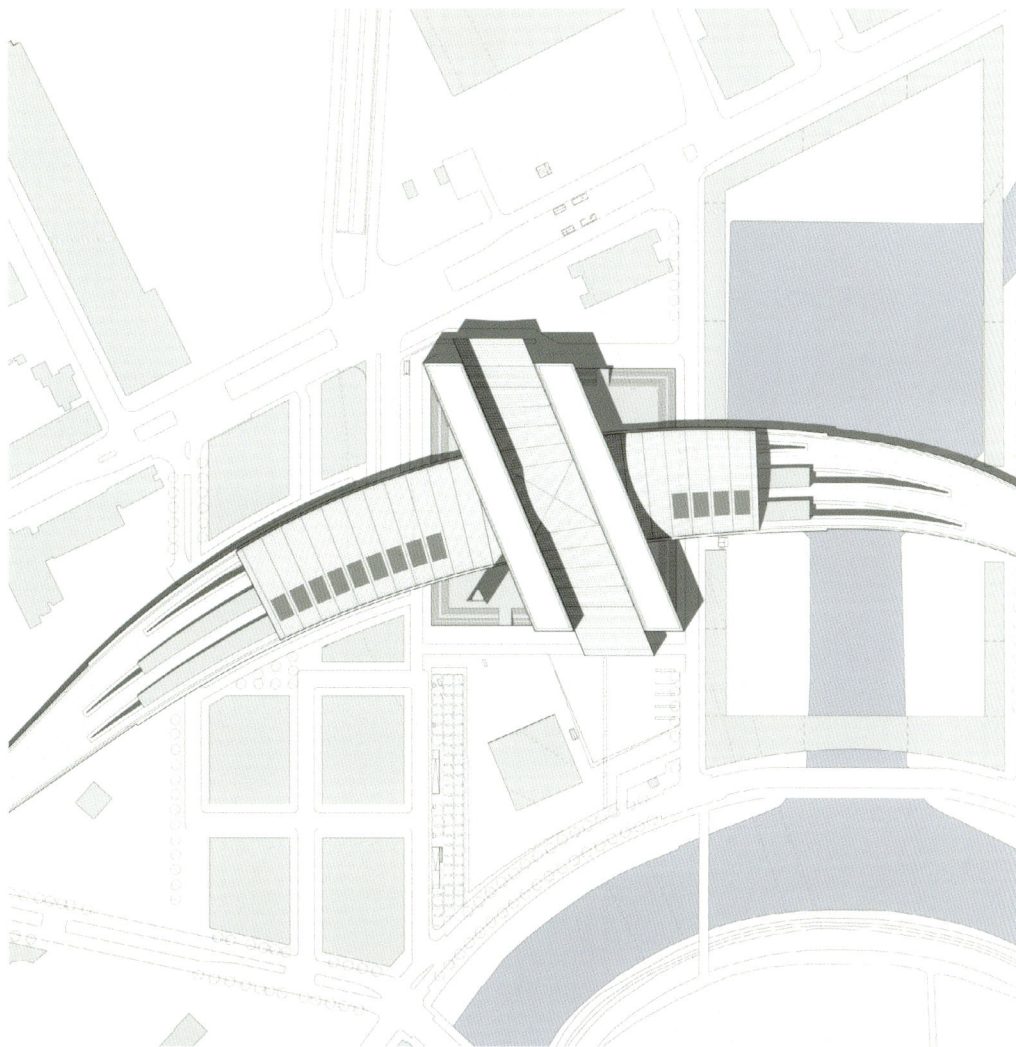

← | **Situation plan**
↓ | **Intersection** of east-west hall and north-south hall form a "crossing"

Benthem Crouwel
Architekten

↑ | **Station square**
↗ | **Aerial view** from the West
→ | **Aerial view** from the North

Station island

Amsterdam

Stations island is to be transformed into an efficient and attractive public transport hub. The station square will be the preserve of pedestrians and trams, purged of all obstacles and paved with granite to provide it with a sense of permanence. Cyclists approaching along the western and eastern flanks can directly access bike parking facilities. Motorized traffic will have its own underpass along the waterfront, overlooked by the new bus terminal. The new IJ Hall presents a natural counterpart to Cuypers' original station concourse and connects with the new neighborhoods along the IJ and in Amsterdam Noord. Here, travelers can effortlessly transfer between bus, metro, train, boat/ferry and taxi.

PROJECT FACTS

Address: Stationsplein, 1012 AB Amsterdam, The Netherlands. **Co architects Masterplan:** Merkx + Girod Architecten (co-architects masterplan). **Client:** City of Amsterdam, Nederlandse Spoorwegen, ProRail. **Completion:** 2015. **Type:** light and heavy rail. **Additional functions:** bus station, public transport by water, shopping, staff facilities. **Main materials:** steel, glass, concrete. **Setting:** inner city.

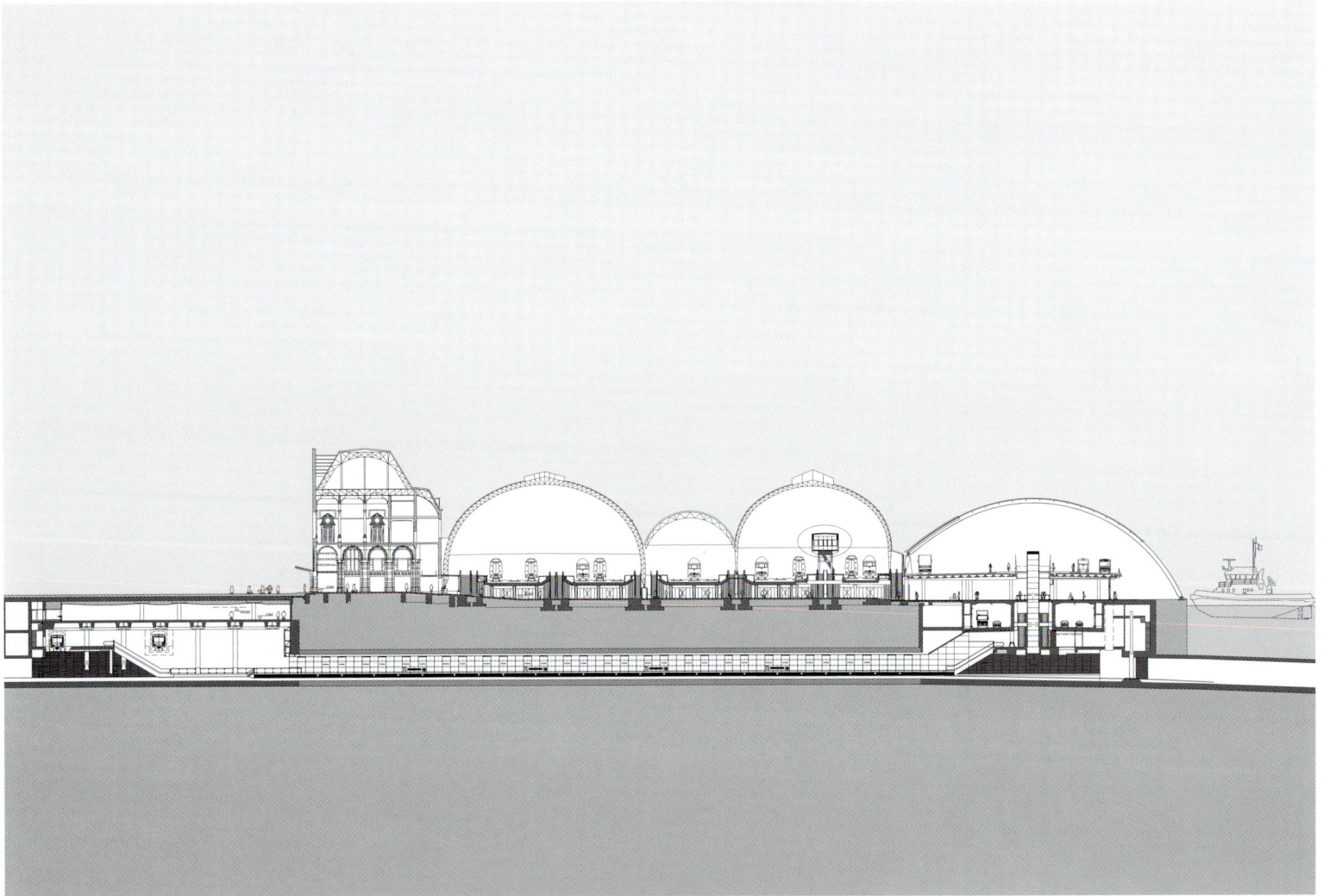

↑ | Section
← | Main hall

← | **View of hall** at the north side
↓ | **View of bus station**

KHR arkitekter /
Anja Rolvung

↑ | **View of the two levels,** regional trains on ground level and metro above
→ | **View of lower platform**

Flintholm station
Copenhagen

The Flintholm station is designed with a passenger capacity of 60,000 in mind, making it one of the largest stations in Denmark. The new, combined station will fulfill very high quality and safety standards, featuring clear passenger routes and shortened distances between different transport systems. The bridges leading up to the station, which is located in a park, were renewed at the same time in order to create a sense of uniformity. The design intended to fuse three stations into one compound to allow passengers to orient inside one single structure. A large glass roof covers the platforms and serves as the projected image and external viewing point of the complex.

Address: Flinthom Allé 55, 2000 Frederiksberg, Denmark. **Planning partner:** Public Arkitekter. **Client:** Banestyrelsen/ DSB. **Completion:** 2004. **Type:** light and heavy rail. **Number of public levels:** 2. **Number of platforms:** 3. **Additional functions:** shopping facilities, parking. **Main materials:** steel, glass, concrete. **Setting:** suburban.

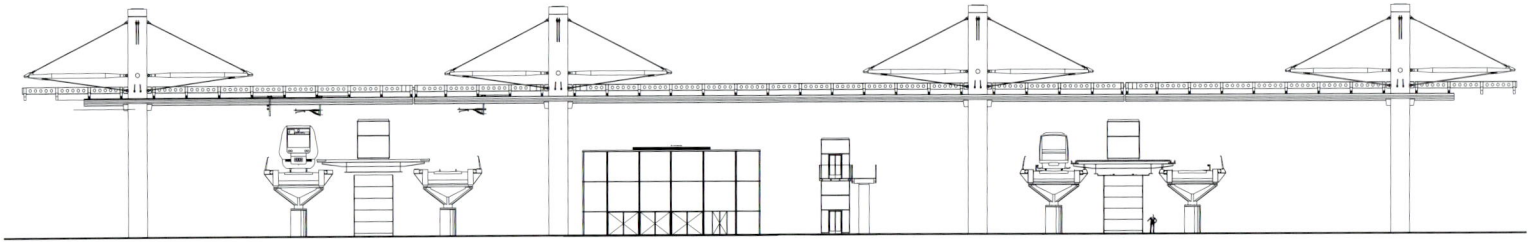

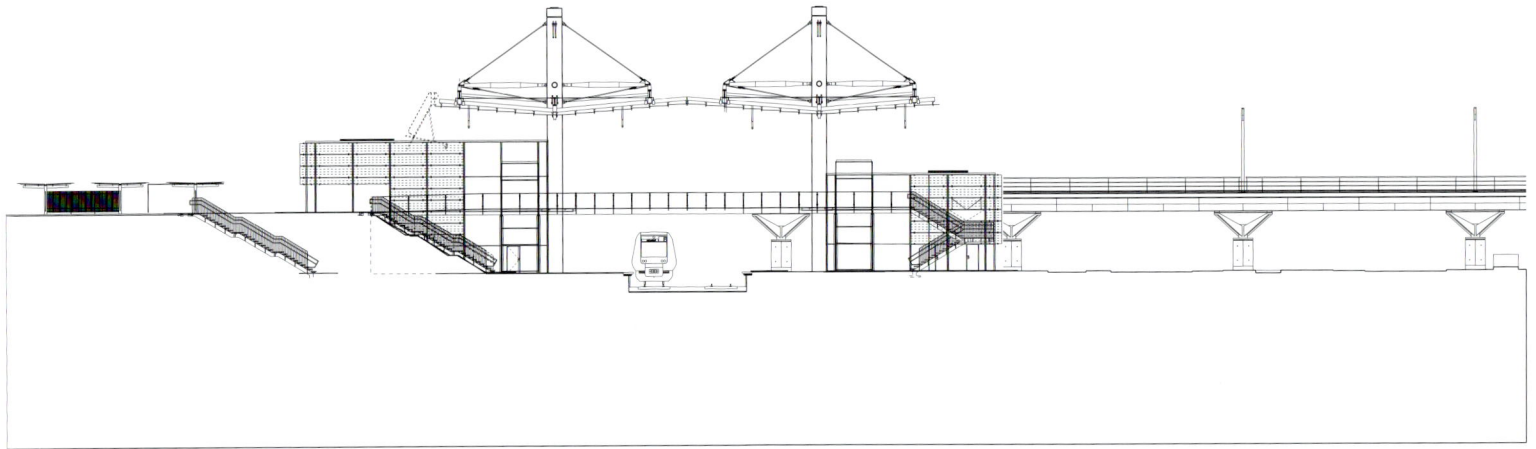

↑ | **Sections**
← | **Detail,** artificial light fixture

← | **Station arrival** at night
↓ | **Perspective** at night

↑ | Main concourse
→ | Entry to subway platform

Sengkang station

Singapore

This station is one of twelve stations comprising Singapore's Northeast Line Expansion. It is designed as a multi-modal station and is located at Sengkang Square, the juncture of a master-planned district. The station includes a mixed-use development, a bus depot, a taxi station, a regional light rail system at the upper level and an MRT subway station below. Simplicity of form and clarity of organization facilitate passenger movement between the station's functions and the adjacent office and residential development. A visual connection to the sun and sky in conjunction with daylight penetration on all levels is maintained by the oval-shaped canopy shielding the roof-level platforms.

PROJECT FACTS

Address: 1 Sengkang Square, Singapore 545078, Singapore. **Planning partner:** 3HP (associate architects), Francis Krahe & Associates Inc. (light consultant). **Client:** Land Transportation Authority. **Completion:** 2004. **Type:** light and heavy rail. **Number of public levels:** 4. **Number of platforms:** 2. **Additional functions:** retail, commercial, office, residential, government, hotel. **Main materials:** glass, stainless steel, granite floors, glass silk screen panels. **Setting:** urban.

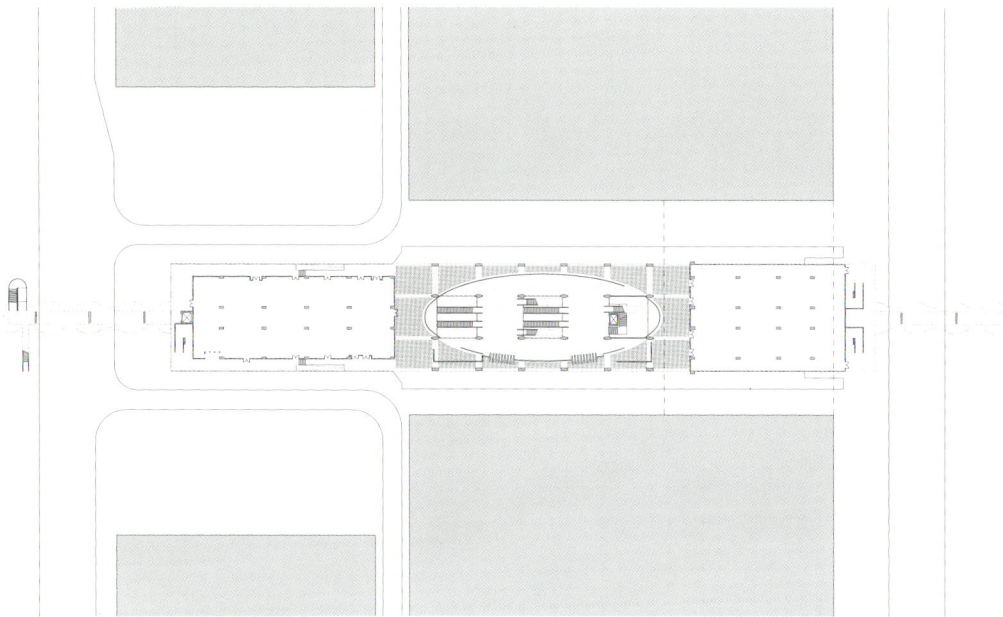

← ← | Vertical transport system
← | Street level plan
↓ | Mezzanine lobby level

TFP Farrells Limited

↑ | **Aerial perspective**
↗ | **Concept sketch**
↗↗ | **Roofs**
→ | **North-south section**

New Guangzhou station

Guangzhou

This station is billed as the largest new station in Asia. It consists of 28 elevated island platforms for intercity and express trains and three underground metro lines with additional allowance for future expansion and interchange to public and private transport systems. The design is based on connecting the local districts of Guangzhou and Foshan on either side of the station and the opportunity afforded by the greenfield site to make this a 'garden' station, which will act as a catalyst for an entirely new urban area. Two landscaped urban plazas constitute the entrances while elevated tracks allow free pedestrian access through a landscaped arrival concourse.

Address: Shibi Village, Guangzhou City, China. **Planning partner:** The Forth Survey and Design Institute of China Railway (FSDI), Beijing Institute of Architectural Design (BIAD). **Interior design:** BIAD. **Client:** Ministry of Railway, China. **Completion:** 2010. **Type:** light and heavy rail. **Number of public levels:** 3. **Number of platforms:** 28. **Number of passengers per day:** 358,500. **Gross floor area:** 495,900 m². **Main materials:** reinforced concrete, steel, glass, granite. **Setting:** suburban.

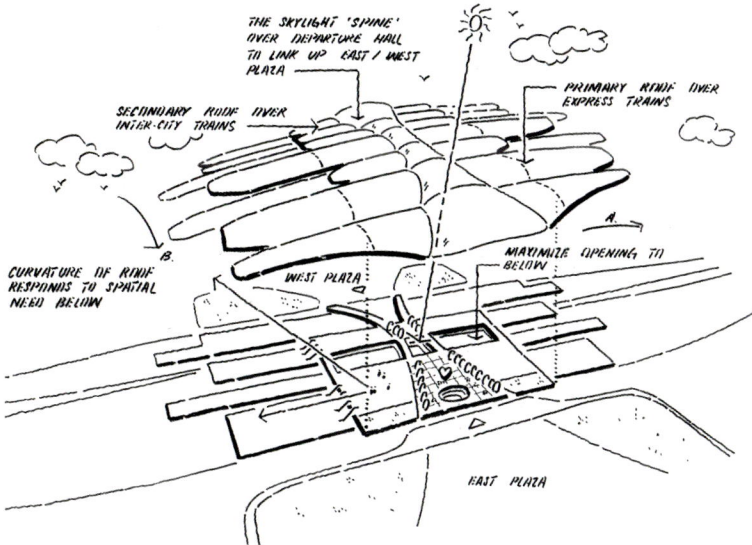

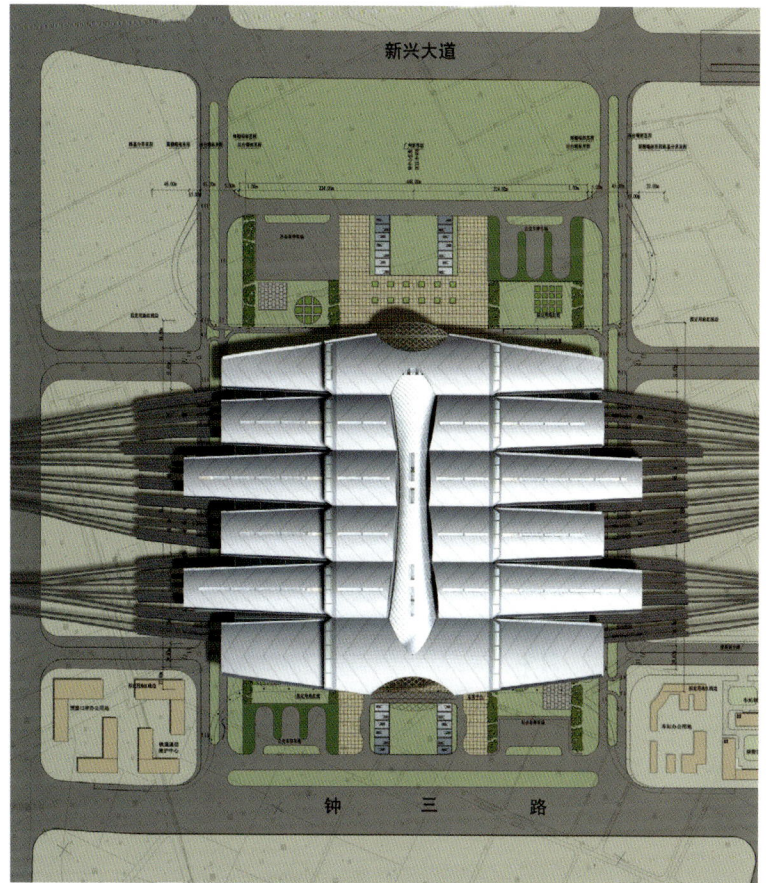

Grimshaw, Arcadis /
Neven Sidor,
Jan van Belkum

↑ | **View along platforms**
→ | **Main concourse** with view towards
staircase to platform level

Bijlmer ArenA station
Amsterdam

This station houses eight train lines and also facilitates easier transfer to metro and bus routes for approximately 60,000 people per day. Grimshaw worked alongside Arcadis in the design of the station which is centered around a 70 meter wide boulevard running east to west, with the tracks and platforms raised on concrete viaducts to provide generous visibility throughout. Two main architectural challenges were faced: to design a station that could be constructed without impinging on the day-to-day operation of the existing facilities, and to create a link through the station between the regenerated area around Amsterdam Arena stadium to the east and major new developments to the west.

PROJECT FACTS **Address:** 1101 Amsterdam Zuid-Oost, The Netherlands. **Client:** ProRail / City of Amsterdam. **Completion:** 2007. **Type:** light and heavy rail. **Number of public levels:** 2. **Number of platforms:** 5. **Number of passengers per day:** 60,000. **Gross floor area:** 6,500 m². **Additional functions:** civic space. **Main materials:** steel, wood panels, concrete. **Setting:** suburban.

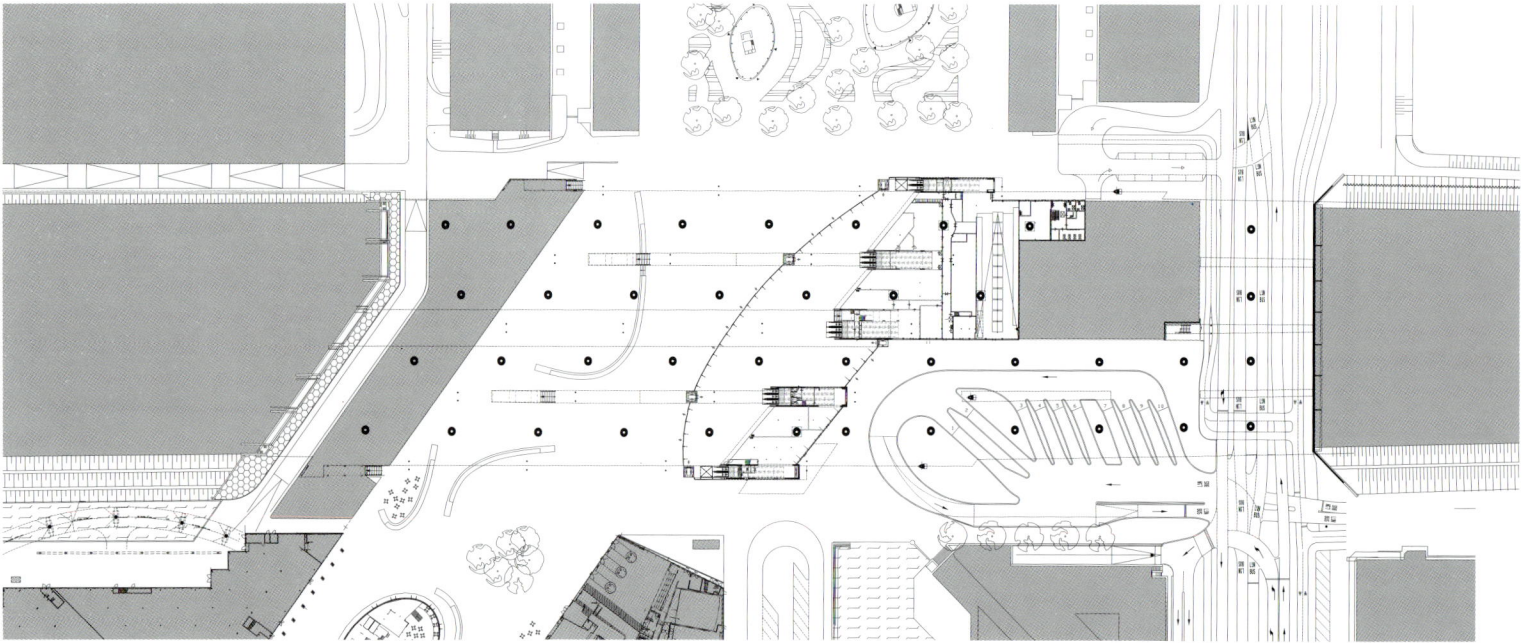

↑ | **Ground floor plan**
← | **View across platforms,** the roof structure rests on angulated columns
→ | **Exterior view**

BDP – Building Design
Partnership Limited /
Peter Jenkins, Peter Shuttle-
worth, Richard Elsdon

↑ | **View of concourse** with heavy rail platforms
→ | **Exterior view** towards entrance at night

Piccadilly station

Manchester

The primary objectives of the Manchester Piccadilly master plan were to overcome passenger and vehicular congestion on the concourse, improve the station as an interchange and gateway to Manchester, and update station parvironment and facilities to 21st century standards. Traffic flow was strategically rerouted to different areas of the complex. The new station buildings utilize a steel frame structure with in-situ concrete floors. The concourse is supported by a concrete transfer structure that sits on the Victorian brick vault and jack arches which previously carried the load of original station buildings, and which still support the existing train shed.

PROJECT FACTS

Address: Station Approach, Manchester, M60 7RA, United Kingdom. **Client:** Network Rail. **Completion:** 2002. **Type:** light and heavy rail. **Number of public levels:** 4. **Number of platforms:** 14. **Number of passengers per day:** 83,000. **Gross floor area:** 20,750 m². **Additional functions:** shopping mall, offices, administration, staff facilities. **Main materials:** exterior: sandstone, glass, steel, ETFE; interior: terrazzo, glass, steel. **Setting:** inner city.

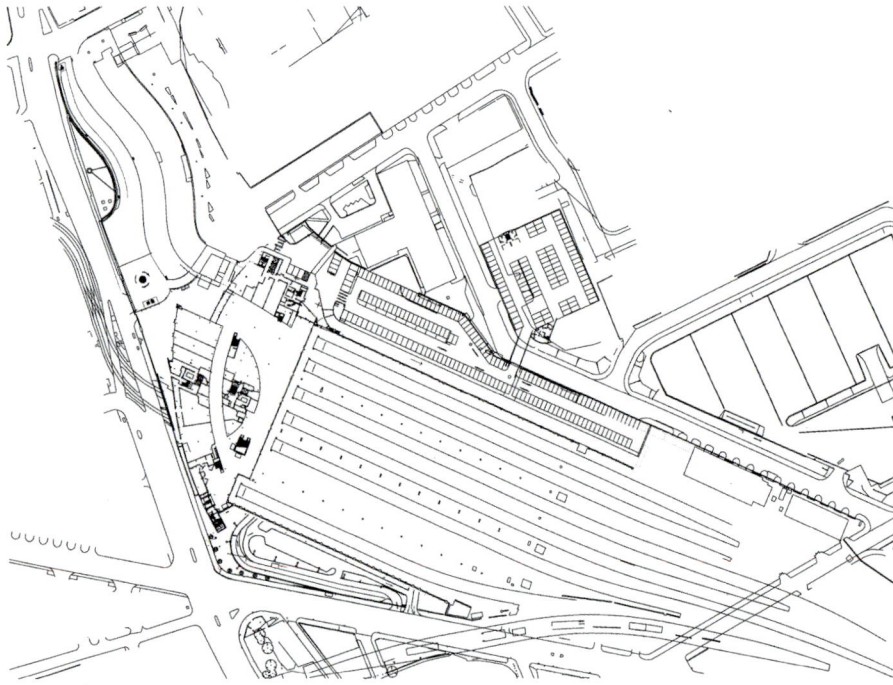

↑ | **Site plan**
← | **Entrance hall** with information screens

← | **View of shopping mall**
↓ | **Entrance hall** with access to the different levels and areas

Mecanoo architecten /
Francine Houben

↑ | **Westside**, by night
↗ | **Station**
→ | **City hall**

Municipal offices and train station
Delft

A railway viaduct which divides the city center in two will be replaced by a railway tunnel, a park, a promenade and a station foyer in combination with offices for over a thousand municipal employees above an underground railway station. The design's starting point was an interweaving of the city's history and its future, resulting in unique relationship of each elevation to its context. Travelers arriving at the station will be greeted by a vaulted ceiling with an image painted in Delft Blue and continued above the city hall, which is separated from the station foyer by a glass wall and a stair and elevator node. Incisions in the building's glass skin form a pattern of alleyways inspired by streets in Old Delft.

PROJECT FACTS

Address: Phoenixstraat, 2611 AM Delft, The Netherlands. **Planning partners:** Benthem Crouwel Architects (Platforms). **Client:** Ontwikkelingsbedrijf Spoorzone, Prorail, Municipality of Delft. **Completion:** 2014. **Type:** light and heavy rail. **Number of public levels:** 1. **Number of platforms:** 4. **Number of passengers per day:** 30,000. **Gross floor area:** station hall: 4,000 m²; city hall ground floor: 2,300 m². **Main materials:** exterior: glass; interior: steel, stucco, ceramic tiles. **Setting:** inner city.

← | **Detail,** ceiling Delft blue
↓ | **Section**

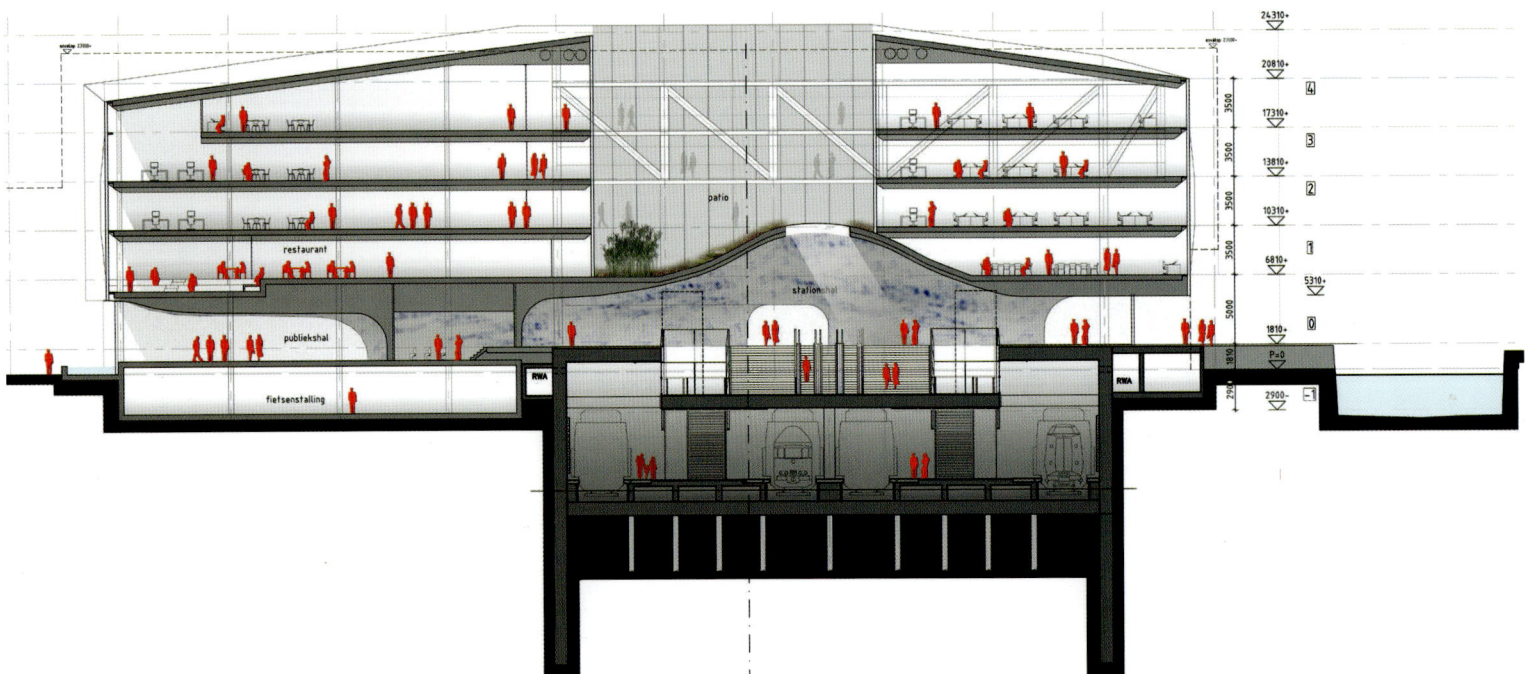

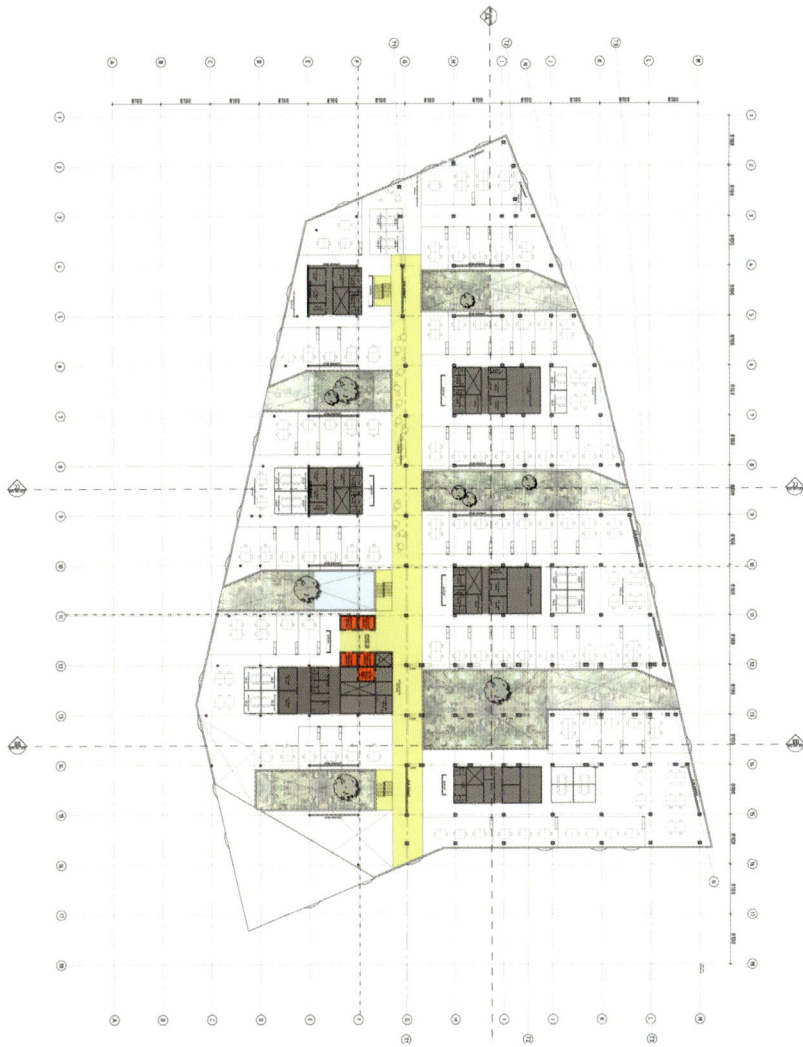

← | **Typical floor plan**
↓ | **View from south**, Coenderstraat

↑ | **Aerial view**
→ | **Interior view**, concourse

Central station

Oslo

The design approach for Oslo's new central station is not only an attempt to create a unified piece of architecture, but a strategic cut into the capital's urban fabric, expanding it in the eastern direction. The architect's ambition was to make the station itself a "pure experience" – a celebration of the concept of travel itself, prioritizing easy orientation, logistic clarity and efficiency. The name "Stasjons Alléen" literally translates as "station boulevard", an open passage through the city. The dynamic steel structure awakens associations of a tree-lined boulevard and creates a gradual transition to surrounding streets, resulting in a natural connection to the city's daily rhythms.

PROJECT FACTS

Address: Jernbanetorget 1, 0154 Oslo, Norway. **Planning partner:** AKT – Adams Kara Taylor / Norconsult (structural engineering), Atkins (traffic planning), Schönherr (landscape planning). **Client:** ROM Eiendom. **Completion:** 2015. **Type:** light and heavy rail. **Number of public levels:** 2. **Number of platforms:** 19. **Number of passengers per day:** 150,000. **Gross floor area:** 80,000 m². **Additional functions:** retail, hotel, office, restaurant, venue. **Main materials:** steel, concrete, glass. **Setting:** inner city.

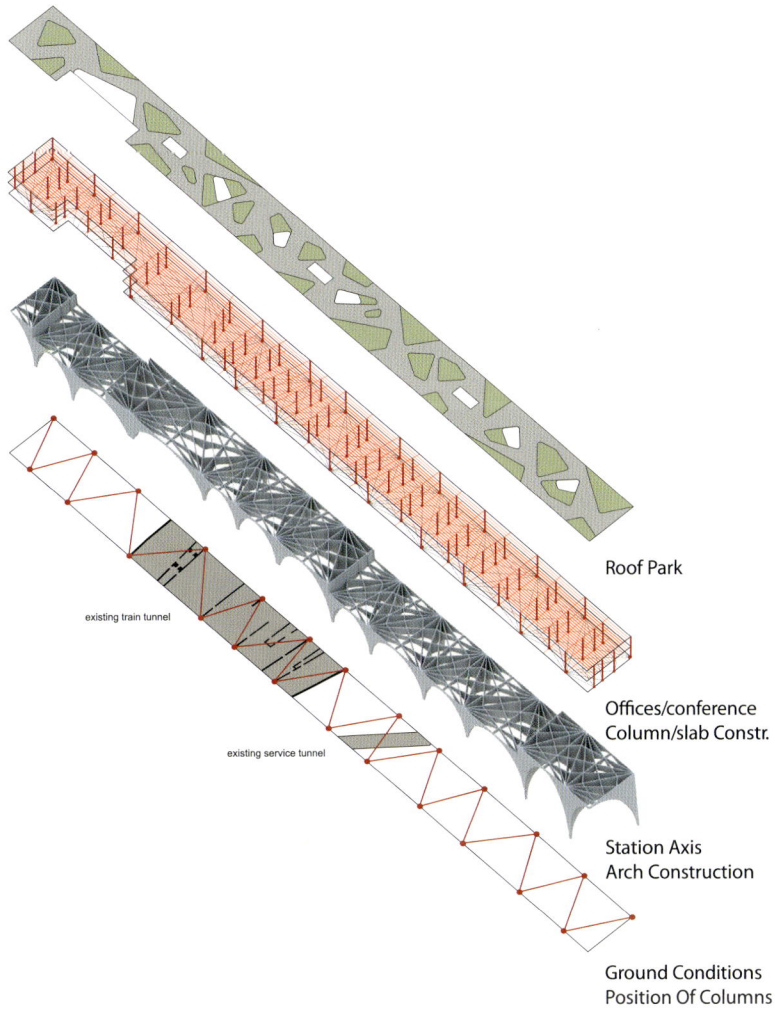

Roof Park

Offices/conference
Column/slab Constr.

Station Axis
Arch Construction

Ground Conditions
Position Of Columns

existing train tunnel

existing service tunnel

←←| Section
↙ | Interior view, showing transition to promenade
← | Structural diagrams
↓ | View from Christian Frederiks Plass

↑ | **Concourse level**
→ | **Platform level**

Buangkok station

Singapore

This suburban station is located in a high-density residential estate and is part of Singapore's Northeast Line Expansion. It is built entirely below grade, with public entrances straddling the high-speed roadway that runs above the station. Taut wings of Teflon-coated fabric protect pedestrians from the elements and lead them into a central public hall that provides shelter for access points and passageways. Inside the station, an open layout and decorated surfaces create a comfortable environment that softens the effects of the underground location and low-hung ceilings required by military regulations.

PROJECT FACTS

Address: 10 Sengkang Center, Singapore 545061, Singapore. **Planning partner:** 3HP (associate architect), Francis Krahe & Associates Inc. (lighting consultant). **Client:** Land Transportation Authority. **Completion:** 2005. **Type:** light and heavy rail. **Number of public levels:** 3. **Number of platforms:** 1. **Additional functions:** residential area, commercial and retail. **Main materials:** steel, Teflon-coated fibre glass, stainless steel panels, glass, granite floor, porcelain silk screen panels. **Setting:** suburban.

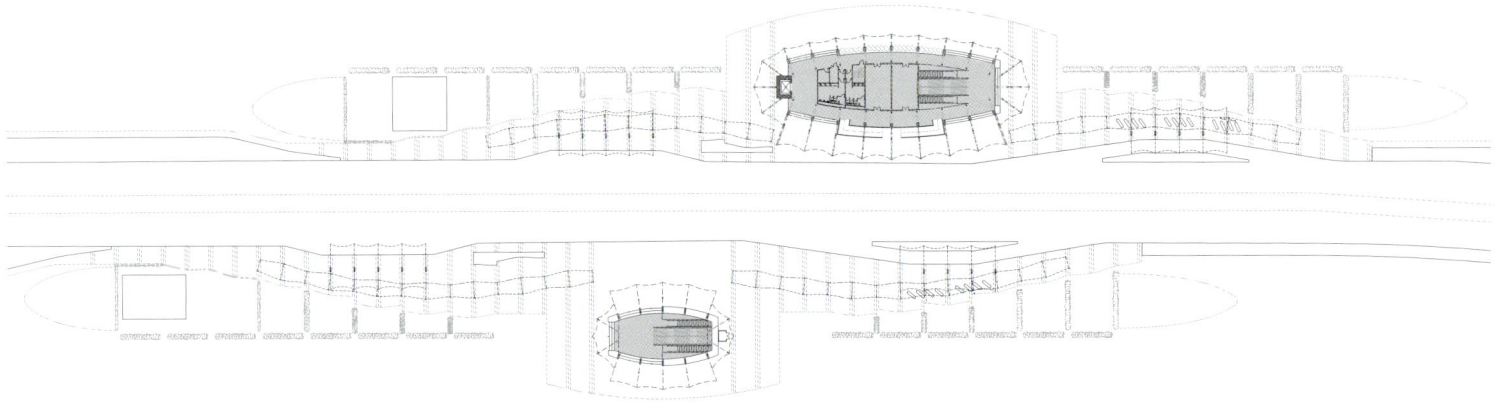

↑ | **Street level plan**
← | **Platform level,** with colorful illustrations
and bright and soft illumination

← | **Drop-off Platform,** with roofed entrance
↓ | **Canopy detail**

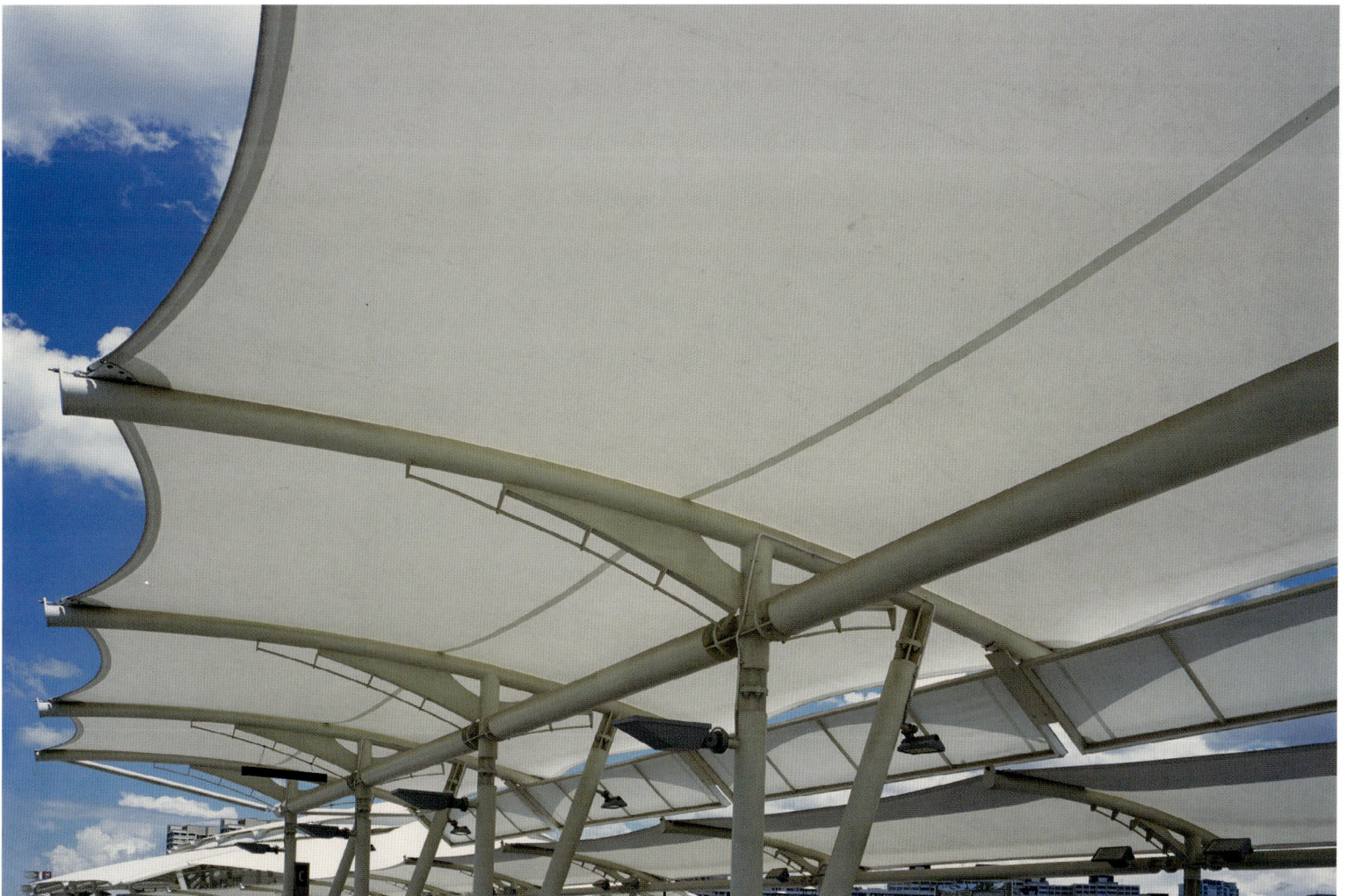

FXFOWLE Architects / Sudhir Jambhekar

↑ | **Entrance hall**
→ | **Entrance**

Roosevelt Avenue intermodal station

New York, NY

This station serves as an entrance and transfer point between the elevated and subgrade subway lines, buses to LaGuardia Airport, and other transit lines for the region. The renovation and expansion of the terminal building provides a modern beacon for the community rooted in the historic infrastructure. The roof's arc brings a graceful line to the utilitarian facility and industrial materials. Various glazing techniques, blue-green terra cotta panels, robust steel detailing, engaging geometry, and clerestory glass murals create a compelling, identifiable civic space. A natural ventilation scheme utilizing the chimney effect replaces an energy-consuming air conditioning system in the iconic hub area.

PROJECT FACTS

Address: Roosevelt Avenue / 74th Street, Queens New York, 11377 NY, USA. **Client:** New York Metropolitan Transportation Authority. **Completion:** 2005. **Type:** light and heavy rail. **Number of public levels:** 5. **Additional functions:** bus station. **Main materials:** glass, steel, concrete. **Setting:** inner city.

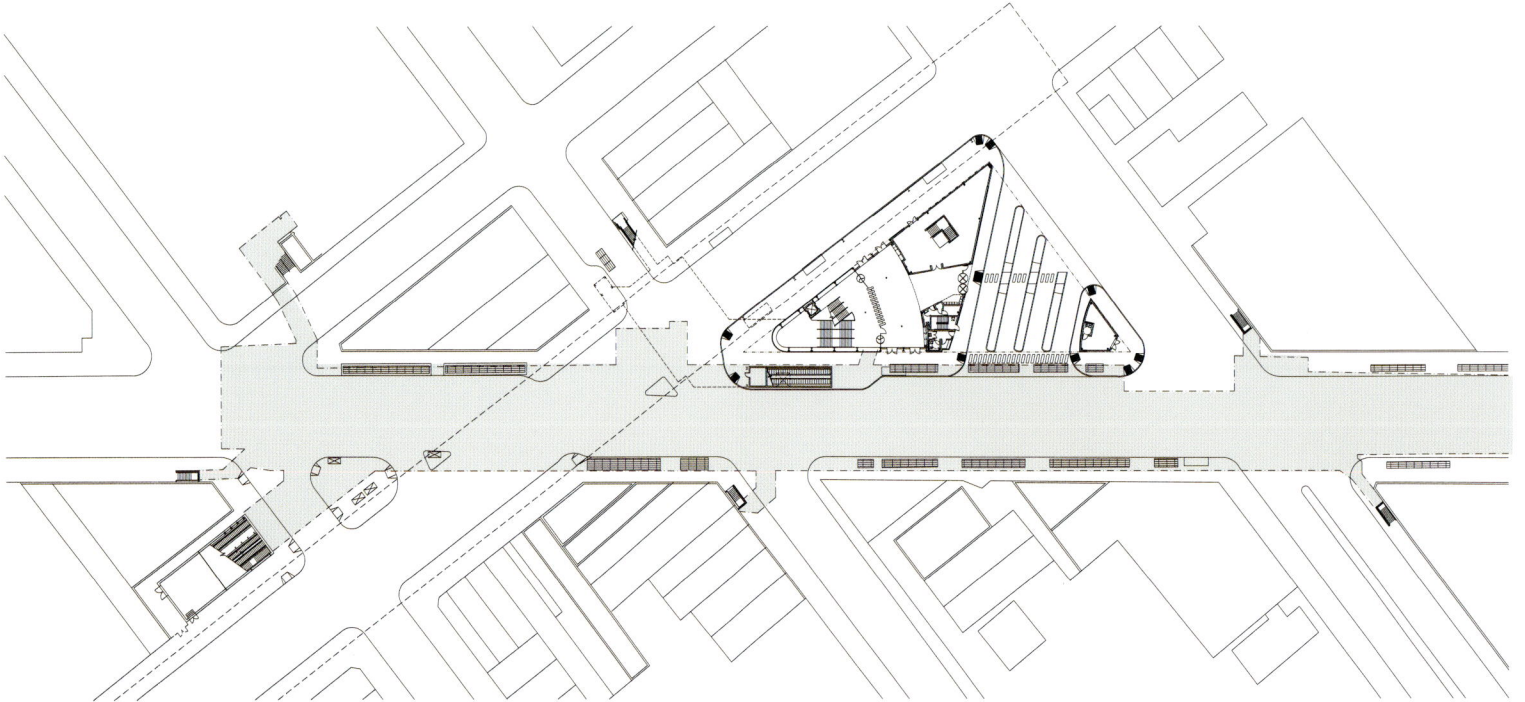

↑ | **Site plan**
← | **Roof structure of the bus terminal** with photovoltaic cells

← | **Terminal building,** view from street level
↓ | **Terminal building,** bird's-eye view

Cruz y Ortiz arquitectos,
Giraudi & Wettstein architetti

↑ | **North-west view,** from above
↗ | **Interior view north to south**
→ | **Access to footbridge** from previous station hall

Redesigning and enlargement of Basel train station

Basel

The silhouette of the roof is visible from various spots in the city, and is a key element in the renovation of the station's image. Underpasses that had joined the platforms were replaced by raised footbridges housing shops gind other facilities, thereby returning lost prominence to the old lobby and connecting separate areas. The roof features slanted planes which converge with existing platform canopies and are broken into almost topographic profiles, giving each functional area a defined height. This way, the roof maintains the continuity of the spatial sequence transversally to the passenger flow, leading to another main hall on the opposite side of the platforms.

PROJECT FACTS

Address: Centralbahnstrasse 10, 4051 Basel, Switzerland. **Client:** SBB – Schweizerische Bundesbahnen AG, Berne. **Completion:** 2003. **Original building:** 1907. **Type:** light and heavy rail. **Number of public levels:** 8. **Number of platforms:** 12. **Number of passengers per day:** 80,000. **Gross floor area:** bridge: 9,000 m², parking: 14,700 m². **Additional functions:** parking, shopping mall. **Main materials:** exterior: metal, glass, interior: stone, glass, wood. **Setting:** urban.

↑ | **Pedestrian south gate entrance**
← | **Floor plan**, footbridge level
↙ | **Floor plan**, platforms level

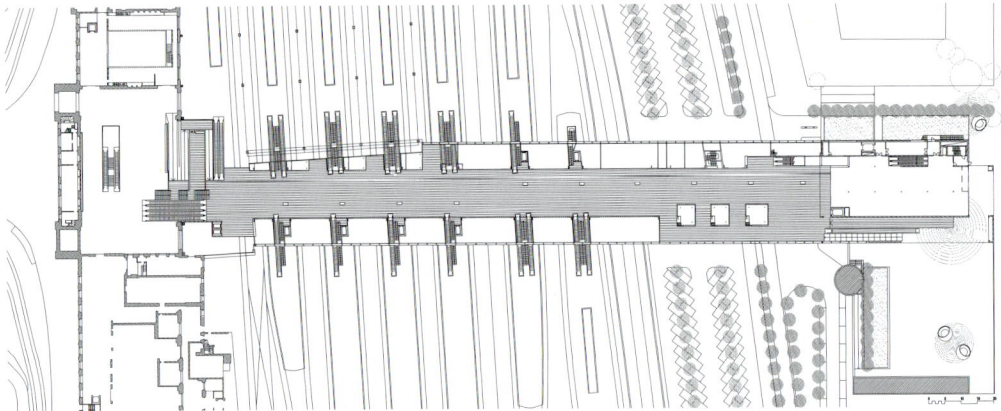

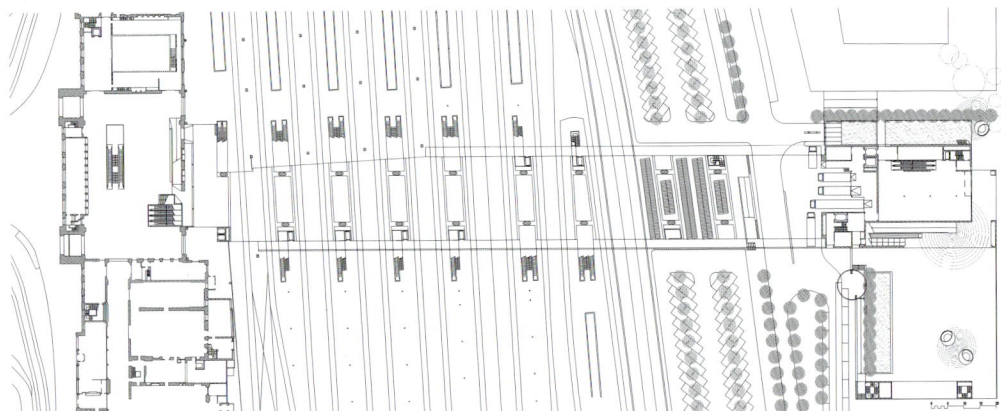

← | **Interior view** from south entrance
↓ | **West view**

↑ | **Entrance façade,** light installation
↗ | **Underpass with shopping mall**
→ | **Station hall**

Station in Zug

Zug

Switzerland's tenth-largest railway station is the successful outcome of intensive and close cooperation of the population, authorities and Swiss railway providers. The station is dominated by the V-shape of the building, a result of the triangular run of the tracks, in conjunction with the elevated location of the two lines on railroad embankments. These constitute a distinctive symbol for the dynamic residential and economic region of Zug. Every evening, however, the hectic station becomes a contemplative arts location, when the entrance façade and the hall are dematerialized through the vivid colors of light artist James Turrell. The work of the architects blends with that of the artist, resulting in an attractive meeting venue as part of the city.

PROJECT FACTS

Address: Bahnhofplatz 1, 6000 Zug, Switzerland. **Light artist:** James Turrell. **Client:** Schweizerische Bundesbahnen SBB, city and and canton of Zug. **Completion:** 2003. **Type:** light and heavy rail. **Number of public levels:** 2. **Number of platforms:** 7. **Number of passengers per day:** 30,000. **Gross floor area:** 8,000 m². **Additional functions:** shopping, offices. **Main materials:** concrete, steel, glass. **Setting:** inner city.

↑ | **Station and station forecourt**
← | **Light installation,** office galleries

← | **Light installation,** view into the hall
↓ | **South façade**
↓↓ | **Section hall**

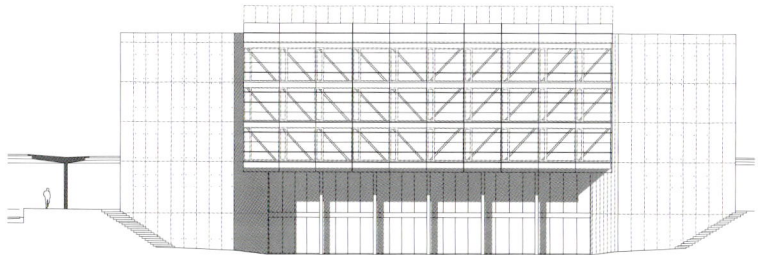

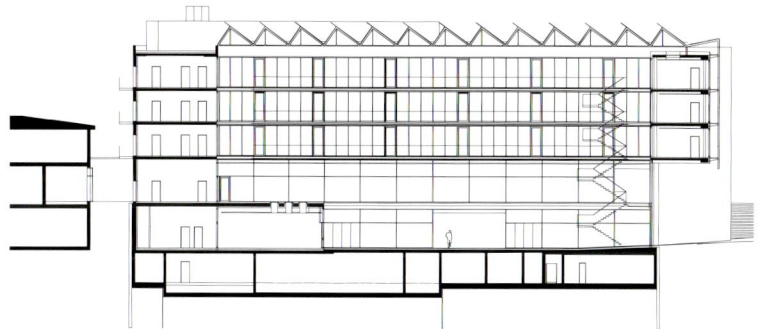

Jörg-Henner Gresbrand,
Dipl.-Ing. Architekt

↑ | **Station area**
↗ | **Bird's-eye view**
→ | **Station forecourt**

Restructuring station area

Rotenburg / Wümme

Located on an area of approximately 10,000 square meters, the station was in dire need for new functional, spatial and design concepts. Measuring approximately 1,350 square meters, the flat slanted roof over the entrance to the tunnel, the bicycle parking area and parts of the service building is at the core of the design. It is completely constructed of steel, bears a photovoltaic system and the slant and decline of its entire 75 meters allows rain water to cascade to the floor. The reflection of uplights illuminates the area located below. Inside the service building along the alignment of the inner city an opening provides a view of the railroad tracks.

PROJECT FACTS

Address: Am Bahnhof 2,4,8, 27356 Rotenburg/W., Germany. **Client:** City of Rotenburg/W. **Completion:** 2009. **Type:** light and heavy rail. **Number of public levels:** 1. **Number of platforms:** 3. **Number of passengers per day:** 3,000. **Gross floor area:** 10,000 m². **Main materials:** wood, steel, tiles. **Setting:** urban.

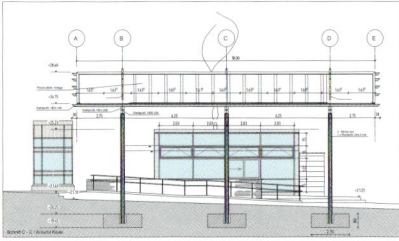

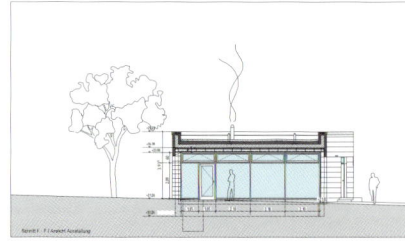

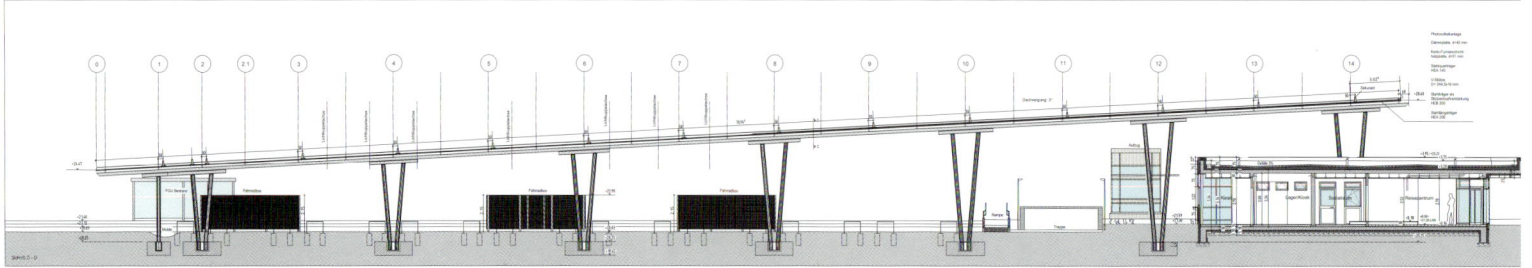

↑ | Sections
← | Platforms

← | **Platform roofing** at night
↓ | **Floor plan**

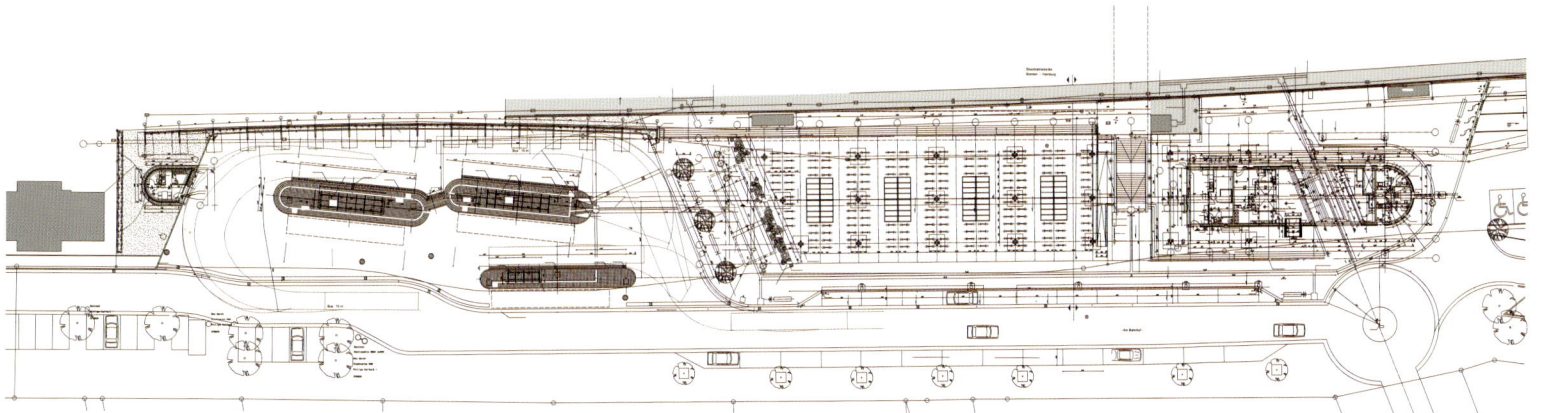

TFP Farrells Limited

↑ | **Station exterior**

New Delhi railway station
New Dehli

The new station and masterplan covers 86 hectares and is designed to replace the current unorganized structure, which currently handles an average of 350,000 passengers a day from 256 trains on 12 platforms. The phasing of the proposed project is critical for redevelopment whilst it is still in full operation. Circulation patterns play a determining role in the architecture, with a segregation of arrivals and departures being essential to prevent cross-flows of pedestrian movement and results in a multilevel design. The overall design incorporates sustainable technology to achieve optimum comfort levels whilst using minimal energy and low cooling loads to reduce energy consumption and costs.

PROJECT FACTS

Address: New Delhi Railway Station, New Delhi, India. **Client:** Ministry of Railway, India. **Completion:** 2016. **Type:** light and heavy rail. **Number of passengers per day:** 350,000. **Number of platforms:** 12. **Gross floor area:** 86 ha. **Main materials:** glass, steel. **Setting:** inner city.

↑ | Aerial view
↙ | Masterplan

↓ | Station interior

↑ | **View of northern entrance**
↗ | **Promenade** towards entrance hall
→ | **Main concourse**

Rotterdam central station

Rotterdam

Rotterdam's new central station is to be re-anchored in the city center and integrated into the European transport hub network, created with the arrival of the high speed rail system (HSL). In the design, the railway zone and city become a single entity by compacting the small-scale surrounding urban fabric. The finer texture, with new sightlines and a mix of residential and commercial space, will greatly improve the zone's social climate. Immediately upon entering the high, light-filled and clearly structured station concourse, travelers are presented with a wide overview of the space. The sunken and widened passage beneath the tracks is a natural continuation of the concourse. Above the platforms is a largely transparent roof which spans the entire track zone.

PROJECT FACTS

Address: Stationsplein 1, 3013 AJ Rotterdam, The Netherlands. **Planning partner:** Meyer en Van Schooten Architecten, West 8 urban design & landscape architecture. **Client:** OntwikkelingsBedrijf Rotterdam. **Completion:** 2013. **Type:** light and heavy rail. **Additional functions:** shopping, offices, restaurant. **Main materials:** steel, glass, concrete. **Setting:** inner city.

↑ | **Interior view** of northern entrance hall
← | **Passage way**

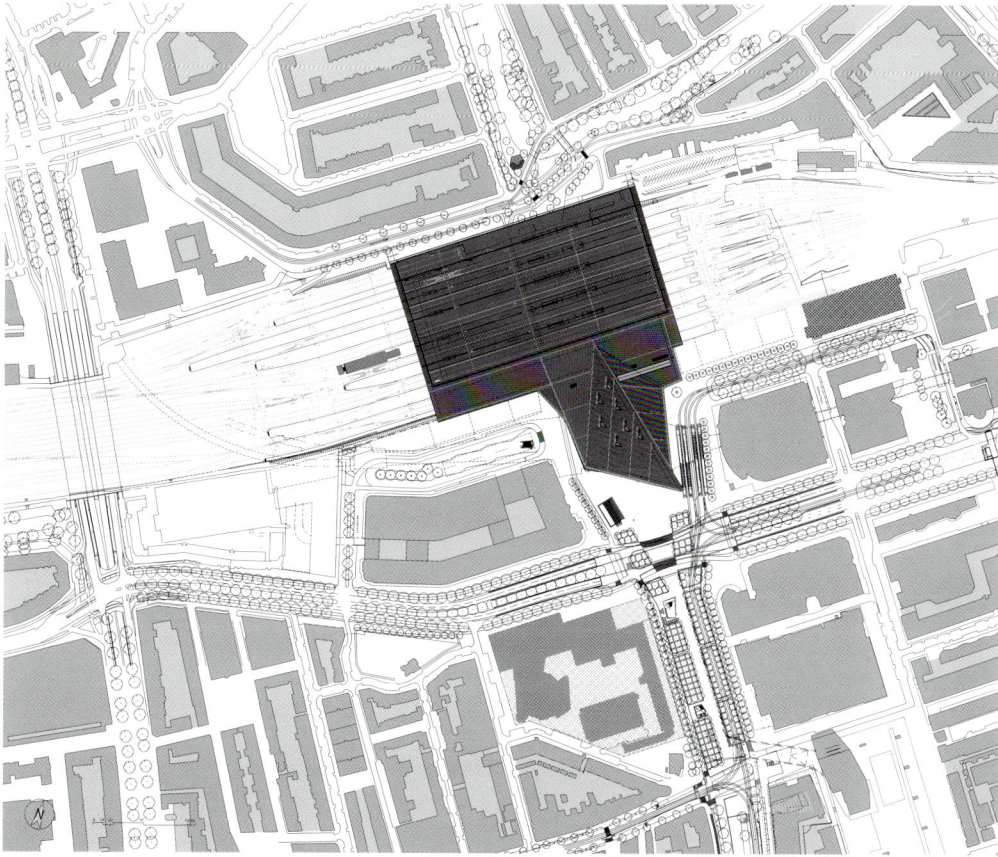

← | **Site plan**
↓ | **Central entrance hall**, general view

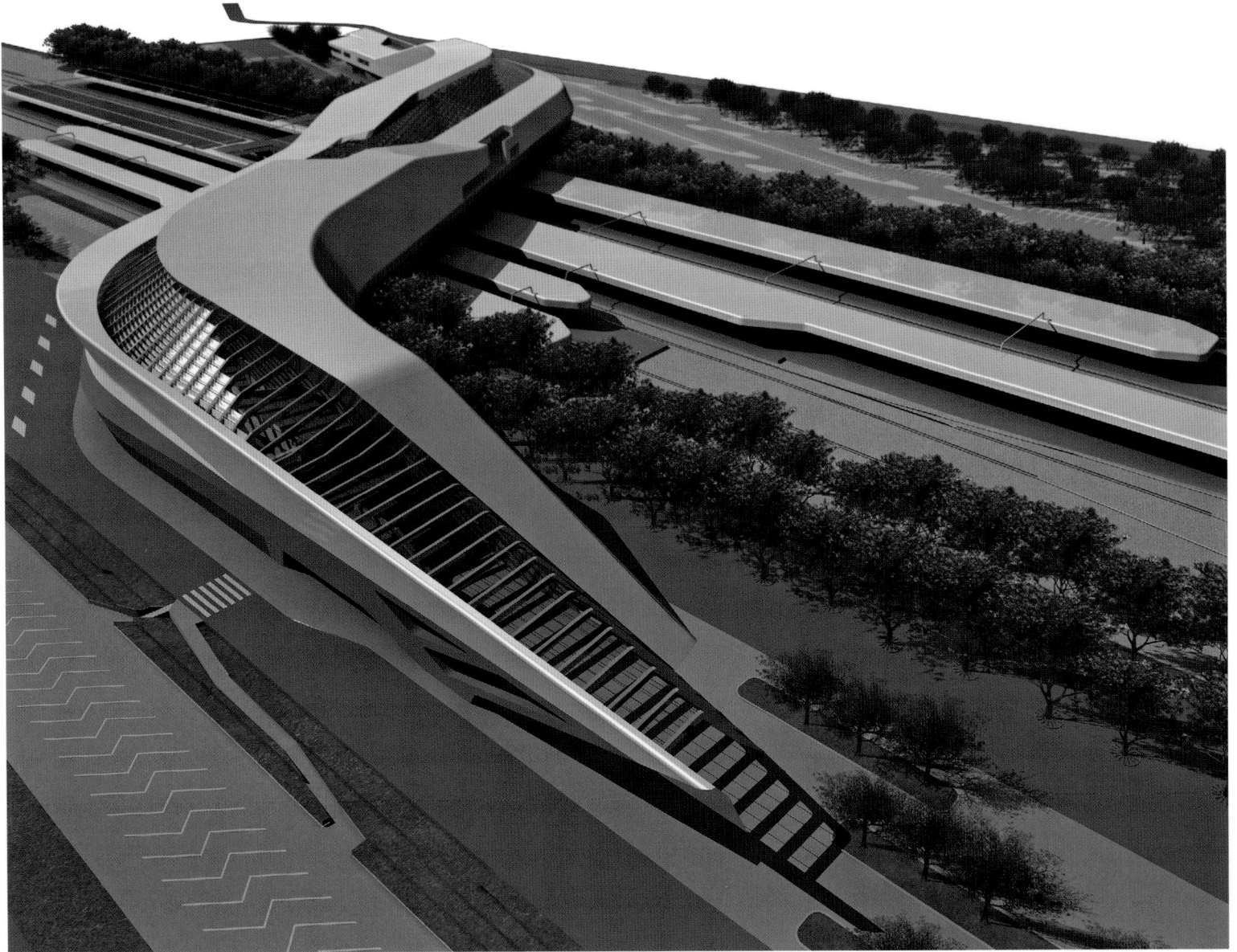

↑ | **Aerial view,** showing the double-bended form of the main corpus
→ | **Interior view,** light and clear atmosphere

Train station Napoli-Afragola

Naples

The new high-speed station is shaped like a bridge which extends across the tracks. The key challenge of the architectural scheme was to create a well-organized transport interchange which would simultaneously serve as a landmark. The concept of the bridge flowed from the idea of enlarging the overhead concourse, which provides access to the numerous platforms, to such a degree that it would turn into the main passenger concourse itself. The bridge concept further allows two strips of extended parkland to move through the site along the tracks, opening and connecting it to the surrounding landscape featuring a business park. The architectural language of the building body as well as its interior focuses on the articulation of movement.

Address: Naples, Italy. **Client:** RFI s.p.a. **Completion:** 2012. **Type:** light and heavy rail. **Gross floor area:** 30,000 m². **Additional functions:** facilities for bus and taxi, police and fire services, mall, public square. **Main materials:** concrete, steel, glass. **Setting:** rural.

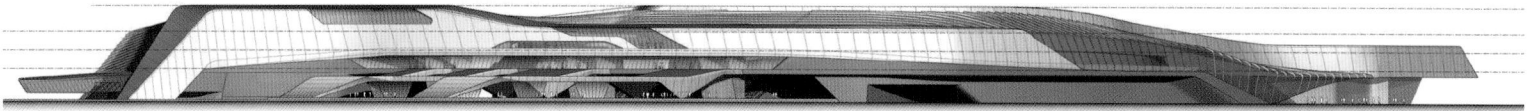

↑ | **Elevations**
← | **General view** from above

← | **Interior view**, ground level
↓ | **Interior view** from second level

↑ | **Overall aerial view**
→ | **Platform level,** with view facing the louvre curtain wall enclosure

Beijing south station
Beijing

Beijing south station was completed in August 2008. This fully integrated multi-modal transportation hub serves as a "gateway" to the capital and a vital link in China's new high-speed intercity rail network. A major urban building and master plan, it is one of the largest contemporary railway stations in the world designed for a passenger turnover of 105 million annually. To accommodate these vast numbers, a new model in railway station design was developed, integrating the multi-modal transport interchange facility with a vertical separation strategy designed so that passenger traffic flows are direct, convenient and highly efficient.

PROJECT FACTS

Address: Kaiyang road, Beijing, China. **Design architect and interior design:** TFP Farrells Ltd in collaboration with Third Railway Survey and Design Institute Group Corporation (TSDI). **Client:** Ministry of Railway, China. **Completion:** 2008. **Type:** light and heavy rail. **Number of public levels:** 3. **Number of platforms:** 24. **Number of passengers per day:** 286,500. **Gross floor area:** 144,190 m². **Main materials:** structure: reinforced concrete, steel; interior: stone cladding, granite, glass, aluminum. **Setting:** urban.

↑ | **Central roof,** composed of a 30,000 m² skylight
← | **Departure level plan**

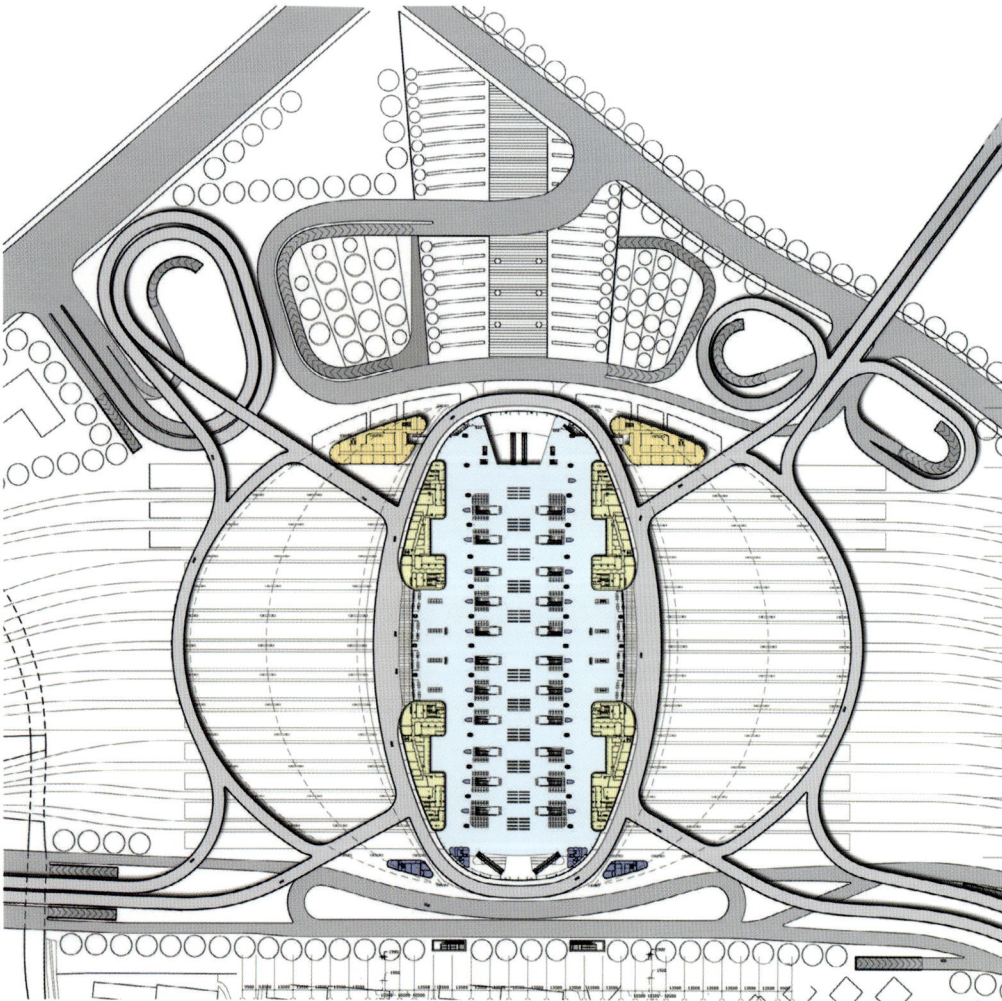

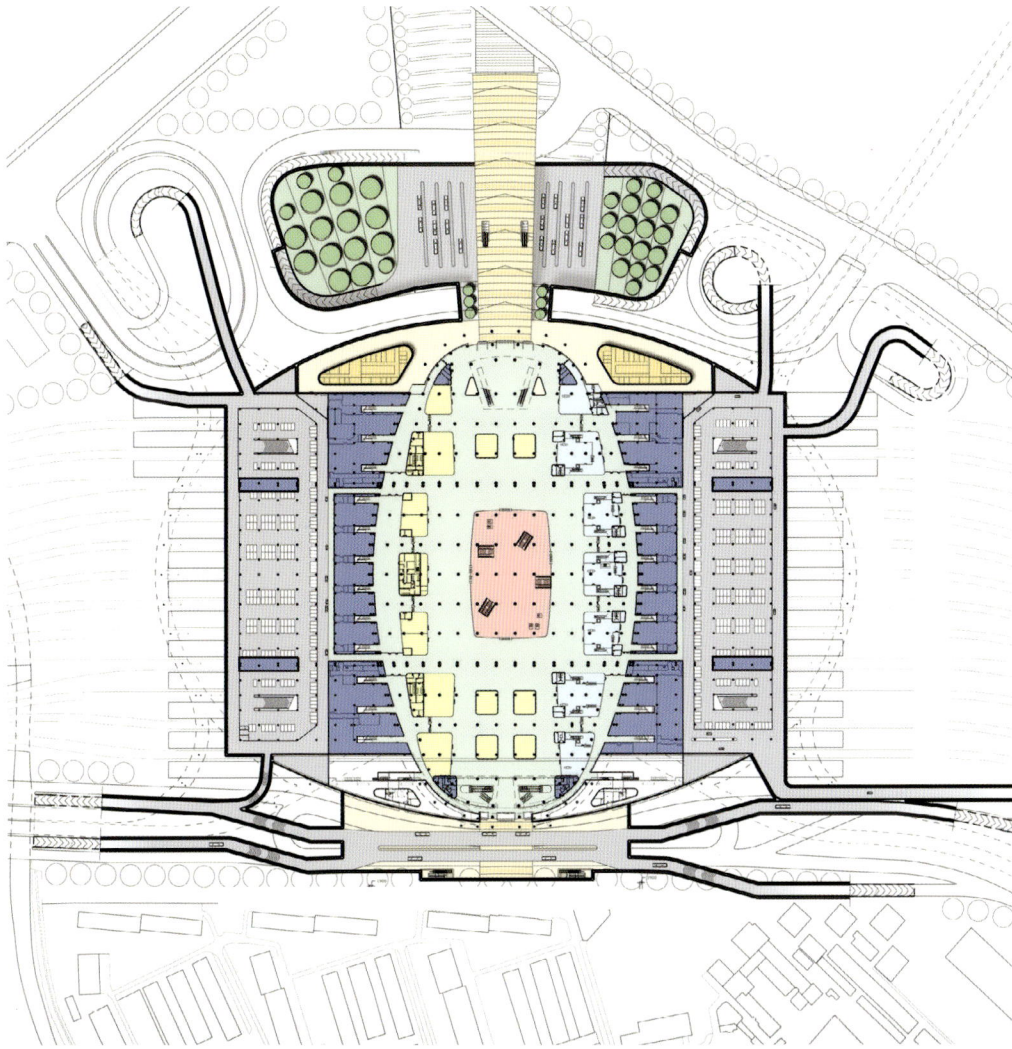

← | **Arrival level plan**
↓ | **On the platforms,** canopy roofs are
permeable to open air for natural ventilation

Index
Arch

itects Index

Atelier 5 Architekten und Planer AG

Sandrainstrasse 3
3001 Berne (Switzerland)
T +41.31.3275252
F +41.31.3275250
atelier5@atelier5.ch
www.atelier5.ch

Aedas

7, Brewery Place, Brewery Wharf, Leeds
West Yorkshire LS10 1NE (United Kingdom)
T +44.113.3858787
F +44.113.3858777
Reception.Leeds@aedas.com
www.aedas.com

Architektengruppe U-Bahn (AGU)

Salmgasse 2
1030 Vienna (Austria)
T +43.1.7121614
F +43.1.7151161
office@agu.at
www.agu.at

Alsop Architects

41 Parkgate Road
London SW11 4NP (United Kingdom)
T +44.20.79787878
F +44.20.79787879
info@alsoparchitects.com
www.alsoparchitects.com

Altoon + Porter Architects

444 South Flower Street, 48th Floor
Los Angeles, CA 90071 (USA)
T +1.213.2251900
F +1.213.2251901
business@altoonporter.com
www.altoonporter.com

Arcadis

P.O. Box 33
6800 LE Arnhem (The Netherlands)
T +31.26.3778911
F +31.26.3515235
info@arcadis-global.com
www.arcadis-global.com

B&M architects Ltd.

Perämiehenkatu 12 E
00150 Helsinki (Finland)
T +358.9.6821102
F +358.9.6927960
jussi.murole@bm-ark.fi
www.bm-ark.fi

BDP – Building Design Partnership Limited

11 Ducie Street, Piccadilly Basin, PO Box 85
Manchester M60 3JA (United Kingdom)
T +44.161.8282200
F +44.161.8282235
manchester@bdp.com
www.bdp.com

Busby Perkins+Will Architects Co.

1220 Homer Street
Vancouver, BC, V6B 2Y5 (Canada)
T +1.604.6845446
F +1.604.6845447
info@busbyperkinswill.ca
www.busbyperkinswill.ca

Santiago Caltrava Architect & Engineer

Parkring 11
8002 Zurich (Switzerland)
T +41.44.2045000
F +41.44.2045001
admin.zurich@calatrava.com
www.calatrava.com

Chapman Taylor

Chapman Taylor LLP
10 Eastbourne Terrace
London W2 6LG (United Kingdom)
T +44.20.73713000
F +44.20.73711949
ctlondon@chapmantaylor.com
www.chapmantaylor.com

→ 44

CollignonArchitektur

Wielandstraße 17
10629 Berlin (Germany)
T +49.30.3151810
F +49.30.31518110
mail@collignonarchitektur.com
www.collignonarchitektur.com

→ 142

Benthem Crouwel Architekten

PO Box 9201
1006 AE Amsterdam (The Netherlands)
T +31.20.6420105
F +31.20.6465354
bca@benthemcrouwel.nl
www.benthemcrouwel.nl

→ 184, 236

Cruz y Ortiz Arquitectos

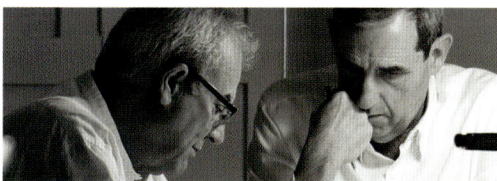

Santas Patronas 36
41001 Seville (Spain)
T +34.954.502825
F +34.954.503704
mail@cruzyortiz.es
www.cruz-ortiz.com

→ 222

Diamond and Schmitt Architects

384 Adelaide Street West, Suite 300
Toronto, ON, M5R 1R7 (Canada)
T +1.416.8628800
F +1.416.8625508
info@dsai.ca
www.dsai.ca

→ 24

EM2N

Josefstrasse 92
8005 Zurich (Schweiz)
T +41.44.2156010
F +41.44.2156011
em2n@em2n.ch
www.em2n.ch

→ 98

FAM Arquitectura y Urbanismo S.L.

Calle Duque de Fernan Nuñez 2
28009 Madrid (Spain)
T +34.91.3690677
correo@estudiofam.com
www.estudiofam.com

→ 62

Foster + Partners

Riverside, 22 Hester Road
London SW11 4AN (United Kingdom)
T +44.20.77380455
F +44.20.77381107
enquiries@fosterandpartners.com
www.fosterandpartners.com

→ 78, 140

FXFOWLE Architects

22 West 19th Street
New York, NY 10011 (USA)
T +1.212.6271700
info@fxfowle.com
www.fxfowle.com

→ 130, 218

Giraudi Wettstein architetti

Via Besso 59
6900 Lugano (Switzerland)
T +41.91.9231423
F +41.91.9210353
info@giraudiwettstein.ch
www.giraudiwettstein.ch

→ 222

gmp – von Gerkan, Marg and Partners Architects

Elbchaussee 139
22763 Hamburg (Germany)
T +49.40.881510
F +49.40.88151177
hamburg-e@gmp-architekten.de
www.gmp-architekten.de

→ 180

Jörg-Henner Gresbrand, Dipl.-Ing. Architekt

Große Straße 1
27356 Rotenburg / Wümme (Germany)
T +49.4261.71161
F +49.4261.71271
jh.gresbrand@rotenburg-wuemme.de

→ 230

Grimshaw

57 Clerkenwell Road
London EC1M 5NG (United Kingdom)
T +44.20.72914141
F +44.20.72914194
info@grimshaw-architects.com
www.grimshaw-architects.com

→ 14, 198

Zaha Hadid Architects

10 Bowling Green Lane
London EC1R 0BQ (United Kingdom)
T +44.207.2535147
F +44.207.2518322
press@zaha-hadid.com
www.zaha-hadid.com

→ 240

Hawkins Brown Architects

60 Bastwick Street
London EC1V 3TN (United Kingdom)
T +44.20.73368030
F +44.20.73368851
mail@hawkinsbrown.co.uk
www.hawkinsbrown.co.uk

→ 168

Hornberger Architekten AG

Englischviertelstrasse 22
8032 Zurich (Switzerland)
T +41.44.2522080
F +41.44.2522081
architekten@hornberger.ch
www.hornberger.ch

→ 226

KHR arkitekter

Kanonbaadsvej 4
1437 Copenhagen (Denmark)
T +45.41.217000
F +45.41.217001
khr@khr.dk
www.khr.dk

→ 188

Kuryłowicz & Associates Architecture

ul. Berezynska 25
03-908 Warsaw (Poland)
T +48.22.6163798
F +48.22.6163799
apaka@apaka.com.pl
www.apaka.com.pl

→ 148

Makoto Sei Watanabe

1-23-30-2806, Azumabashi, Sumida-ku
Tokyo 130-0001 (Japan)
F +81.3.38293837
are@makoto-architect.com
www.makoto-architect.com

→ 18, 28, 48

Mecanoo architecten

PO Box 3277
2601 DG Delft (The Netherlands)
T +31.15.2798100
F +31.15.2798111
info@mecanoo.nl
www.mecanoo.nl

→ 206

MJP Architects

9 Heneage Street
Spitalfields, London E1 5IJ (United Kingdom)
T +44.20.73779262
F +44.20.72477854
mjp@mjparchitects.co.uk
www.mjparchitects.co.uk

→ 150

Hans Moor Architects

Vasteland 8
3011 BK Rotterdam (The Netherlands)
T +31.10.4123344
F +31.10.4334439
info@hansmoor.nl
www.hansmoor.nl

→ 94

Architekt Moßburger

Jacquingasse 29
1030 Vienna (Austria)
T +43.1.7991545
F +43.1.799154594
office@mossburger.at
www.mossburger.at

→ 160

Ateliers Jean Nouvel

10 Cité d'Angoulême
75011 Paris (France)
T +33.1.49238383
F +33.1.43148110
info@jeannouvel.fr
www.jeannouvel.com

→ 102

ON-A

c/ Doctor Rizal 8, Local 1
08008 Barcelona (Spain)
T +34.93.2184306
F +34.93.2184306
contact@on-a.es
www.on-a.es

→ 174

Osterwold°Schmidt EXP!ANDER Architekten BDA

Brühl 22
99423 Weimar (Germany)
T +49.3643.7736580
F +49.3643.7736581
mail@osterwold-schmidt.de
www.osterwold-schmidt.de

→ 110

Pahl + Weber-Pahl Planungsgesellschaft

Spreestraße 3
64295 Darmstadt (Germany)
T +49.6151.314705
F +49.6151.314706
info@pahl-architekten.de
www.pahl-architekten.de

→ 92

Rogers, Stirk, Harbour + Partners

Thames Wharf, Rainville Road
London W6 9HA (United Kingdom)
T +44.20.73851235
F +44.20.73858409
enquiries@rsh-p.com
www.rsh-p.com

→ 144

Sasaki Associates

64 Pleasant Street
Watertown, MA 02472 (USA)
T +1.617.9263300
F +1.617.9242748
info@sasaki.com
www.sasaki.com

→ 126

Schoyerer Architekten BDA

Hauptstraße 17–19
55120 Mainz (Germany)
T +49.6131.288481
F +49.6131.288488
architekten@schoyerer.de
www.schoyerer.de

→ 84

smarch – Mathys & Stücheli Architekten

Neuengasse 41
3011 Berne (Switzerland)
T +41.31.3129600
F +41.31.3129601
smarch@smarch.ch
www.smarch.ch

→ 36

Space Group

Hausmannsgate 16
0182 Oslo (Norway)
T +47.22.038888
F +47.22.201074
info@spacegroup.no
www.spacegroup.no

→ 210

SPORAARCHITECTS

Hutyra Ferenc u. 11–15
1074 Budapest (Hungary)
T +36.1.2253530
F +36.1.2253529
spora@sporaarchitects.hu
www.sporaarchitects.hu

→ **156**

Arch. DI. Albert Wimmer

Flachgasse 53
1150 Vienna (Austria)
T +43.1.9823000
F +43.1.982300030
office@awimmer.at
www.awimmer.at

→ **114**

Zwarts & Jansma Architects

Vijzelstraat 270
1017 Amsterdam (The Netherlands)
T +31.20.5352200
F +31.20.5352211
post@zwarts.jansma.nl
www.zwarts.jansma.nl,

→ **74, 134**

Edward Suzuki Associates

Keyaki House 101, 19-10, 3-chome Nishi-Azabu,
Minato-ku
Tokyo 106-0031 (Japan)
T +81.3.57705395
F +81.3.57705397
iesa@edward.net
www.edward.net

→ **88**

WOHA

29 Hongkong Street
Singapore 059668 (Singapore)
T +65.6423.4555
F +65.6423.4666
pr@wohadesigns.com
www.wohadesigns.com

→ **40, 66**

TFP Farrells Limited

4th Floor, St John's Building, 33 Garden Road
Central Hong Kong (China)
T +852.2523.0183
F +852.2596.0216
tfp@tfp-hk.com
www.tfpfarrells.com

→ **196, 234, 244**

ZGF Architects LLP

1223 SW Washington Street, Suite 200
Portland, OR 97205 (USA)
T +1.503.2243860
F +1.503.2242482
info@zgf.com
www.zgf.com

→ **164**

IMPRINT

The Deutsche Nationalbibliothek lists this publication in
the Deutsche Nationalbibliografie; detailed bibliographical
data are available on the internet at http://dnb.d-nb.de.

ISBN 978-3-03768-044-5

© 2010 by Braun Publishing AG
www.braun-publishing.ch

1st edition 2010

Project coordination: Editorial office van Uffelen
Text editing: Marek Heinel, Chris van Uffelen
Editiorial staff: Anika Burger
Translation: Alice Bayandin, Cosima Talhouni
Graphic concept: ON Grafik | Tom Wibberenz
Layout: Marek Heinel, Georgia van Uffelen
Reproduction: Bild1Druck GmbH, Berlin